Action Research for Teachers

A practical guide

Other titles of interest . . .

The Art of Action Research in the Classroom
Christine Macintyre
1-85346-701-4

Foundations of Primary Teaching (Third Edition)
Denis Hayes
1-84312-131-X

Early Professional Development for Teachers
Frank Banks and Ann Shelton-Mayes
1-84346-792-8

Get Their Attention!
How to Gain Pupils' Respect and Thrive as a Teacher
Sean O'Flynn, Harry Kennedy and Michelle MacGrath
1-84312-080-1

Putting Research into Practice in Primary Teaching and Learning
Suzi Clipson-Boyles
1-85346-642-5

Teacher-Led Development Work
Guidance and Support
David Frost and Judy Durrant
1-84312-006-2

Subject Leadership in the Primary School
A Practical Guide for Curriculum Coordinators
Joan Dean
1-84312-083-6

Action Research for Teachers

A practical guide

Jean McNiff and Jack Whitehead

 David Fulton Publishers

David Fulton Publishers
2 Park Square, Milton Park, Abingdon, Oxon OX14 4RN

270 Madison Avenue, New York, NY 10016

David Fulton Publishers is an imprint of the Taylor & Francis Group, an informa business

British Library Cataloguing in Publication Data
A catalogue record for this book is available from the British Library.

ISBN: 1 84312 321 5

Typeset by RefineCatch Limited, Bungay, Suffolk

Contents

Acknowledgements

We wish to thank Máirín Glenn and Mary Roche for their painstaking reviews of the manuscript and very helpful suggestions.

Thank you also to Margaret Marriott, our editor at David Fulton Publishers, whose encouragement sustained us throughout.

Special thanks are due to our colleagues, those whose work is reproduced and cited here, and those others whose work contributes to educational sustainability.

Jack expresses his thanks in these words:

Thanks for the pleasure in sharing the flow of our life-affirming energies in values that carry hope through our life and work.

Jean expresses her thanks in these words:

Thanks, and remember me, O my God, for good. (Nehemiah, 13 : 31)

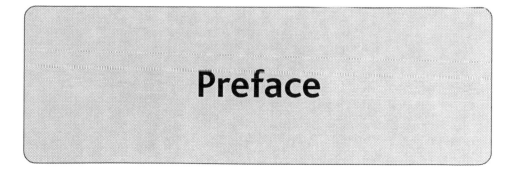

Preface

This book is about doing action research in schools and colleges. It is written for teachers, regardless of their official role or responsibility, who are trying to find ways through education to improve their lives and the world we live in.

Many books on action research are available today. Most explain what action research is and how it can be done. This book also explains what action research is, and gives practical advice about how you can do it, for yourself, in your own context. We encourage you to ask questions and test any provisional answers, and we offer ideas and guidance that will enable you to decide for yourself what to do. Our aim is to encourage you to see that, whatever is said about action research, you can do it too. You can, and should, be a teacher-researcher. There is nothing too difficult about doing research. It strengthens the discipline and rigour in what we are already doing. It can also be exciting and rewarding, and it can bring benefit to many people, including yourself.

The book is a short practical guide that talks mainly about the 'what' and 'how' of doing action research. It touches only briefly on the 'why', because we have written about these things elsewhere. You can find further information, help and resources in our other books and papers, and on our websites. Jack's address is http://www.actionresearch.net and Jean's is http://www.jeanmcniff.com. If you write to us, we will respond.

We do urge you to do your own action research, and to find ways of connecting with other practitioners across the professions and around the world. There is no greater power for world sustainability than groups of educators who come together to achieve their democratically negotiated social and educational goals. We speak from experience. We are part of global networks of communities of practitioner-researchers who are working together for a better future today. You can be there too.

Jean McNiff and Jack Whitehead

What is action research and why should you do it?

Action research is a common-sense approach to personal and professional development that enables practitioners everywhere to investigate and evaluate their work, and to create their own theories of practice. They ask, 'What am I doing? How can I check that I am doing it well? How can I do it better? How can others and I learn together?' It has become increasingly popular around the world in professional learning contexts, especially in the teaching profession. Teachers are able systematically to investigate what they are doing, individually and collectively, in order to make sure that their work is as they want it to be. They can do this by asking practical questions such as:

- What is my concern?
- Why am I concerned?
- What kind of evidence can I produce to show why I am concerned?
- What can I do about it?
- What will I do about it?
- What kind of evidence will I produce to show how the situation is unfolding?
- How do I make sure that any conclusions I come to are reasonably fair and accurate?
- How do I modify my practice in the light of my evaluation?

These questions are developed in Chapter 2.

What is special about action research?

Action research is practical. It is so practical that when people first meet the idea they often say, 'That's what I do in any case. What's different?'

What is different is that action research insists on teachers justifying their claims to knowledge by the production of authenticated and validated evidence, and then making their claims public in order to subject them to critical evaluation. In this sense, it is also different from action learning, which tends to focus on action but not always on testing knowledge claims. A claim to knowledge is the term used for when we say we have learned something, or now believe something to be the case, or when we reconfigure existing knowledge to create new knowledge. This means that when people begin to investigate their work, they need systematically to monitor what they are doing, gather data, and find ways of making judgements about it in order to generate evidence. They use this evidence to support their claims to knowledge. Therefore, if you as a teacher believe you are justified in saying that you have influenced the quality of children's learning, you would need to produce evidence to support that claim. If as a principal you say that you have negotiated a more democratic way of working in school (as Mark Potts does in his 2002 study), you would need to produce evidence from teachers, parents and students to support what you say. Chapters 4 and 5 are all about gathering data and generating evidence. Without evidence, your claim to knowledge could be construed as your opinion or even your wishful thinking.

How is action research used and who does it?

Action research is used widely in the initial and continuing professional learning of teachers and other professionals. One of the attractions is that everyone can do it, so it is not only teachers in schools who investigate their work but also principals, heads of department and administrators – indeed, anyone who regards their work as teaching. Students also do, and should do, action research (Steinberg and Kincheloe 1998). Teachers and students working together can form powerful communities of educational practice (Wenger 1998).

Why should teachers do action research?

There are two main reasons for doing action research:

- to improve practices
- to generate new theory.

Much of the action research literature focuses on how and why teachers can improve practices, which is of course crucial, but not enough. It is also vital to show how action research generates new theory. Here is why.

Action research has been around for a long time, and different people have different ideas about how it should be done. Some people think it is enough for an external researcher to tell other people, including teachers, what to do. We (Jack and Jean) do not share this view. Like many others, we believe that teachers are best placed to make professional judgements about evaluating and improving their own work. Teachers can, and should, ask, 'How do I improve what I am doing?', and demonstrate that they know what they are doing, why they are doing it, and for what purpose. This idea that teachers are best placed to make judgements about their own work is accepted widely, to the extent that teachers are authorised to take main responsibility for their initial and continuing professional learning. Recognition of their practical expertise has done much to enhance teachers' professional status, and is manifested in different ways, such as in the changed relationship between themselves and higher education institutions (HEIs). Whereas previously the work of HEIs was to pass on received wisdom about practice, now teachers themselves make decisions about their own practice.

Something is still missing. The recognition works largely in relation to practice and not so much in relation to theory, or knowledge creation. This is a major issue, because theory generation is at the heart of the policy making that provides new directions for the profession. Teachers are still seen as expert practitioners, not as expert knowers, which is a concern, because teachers need to have a say in what counts as policy. To do so they need to have confidence in themselves as creators of new theory, so that other people also will develop confidence in their capacity. However, teachers are sometimes heard to say that they are not particularly interested in theory. This may be because theory is often (perhaps deliberately) presented as a body of abstract knowledge that teachers are expected to access and apply. Teachers also tend to be suspicious of the idea of research, again not surprisingly, because many have experienced being used by an official researcher as objects of investigation or sources of data. This is why action research is so valuable. It is done by people who are studying themselves and their work, and asking questions about what they are doing, why they are doing it, and how they can improve it – a practical, systematic form of enquiry, with the emphasis on what is happening in everyday work. We believe that teachers are powerful creators of theory and should be recognised as such. Getting recognition, however, means developing confidence in one's own capacity for doing research.

Doing action research

There is nothing mysterious about doing research. It is a systematic, disciplined process of finding out something that was not known before, showing that the new knowledge is valid, and subjecting it to the critical evaluation of other people. There is also nothing mysterious about the idea of theory. We all have theories about how things work. Theory is not only an abstract body of knowledge 'out there', which is one kind of theory but also is located in teachers' professional experience 'in here', which is another kind of theory. When you are faced with one of the thousands of decisions you have to make every time you meet with your class, you draw on your vast repertoire of knowledge and expertise. Your knowledge and expertise make up your theories of practice, that is, how you understand what you do and why you do it. We all have theories about the way things should be, and these guide our actions. When you make a decision, you draw on your existing theories and also produce new theories. When you ask in a split second, 'Should I do this or that? Why? What might be the implications?', you are creating a new theory of practice.

Many teachers, however, talk about their work only as 'what we do' (practice) rather than as 'how we understand what we do' (theory), seeing practice as informed by common sense or practical wisdom, nothing special, what good teachers do in any case. Talking about practice as activity, rather than as considered, committed and purposeful action (praxis), presents teachers as implementers of practice but not theorists of practice. Theorists still tend to be seen as people in higher education, who produce abstract knowledge, which teachers apply to their practice.

This is where action research comes in. Action research can help people to improve their practice, and it can also help people to see their practice as practical theorising. There is no separation of practice and theory. Practice (what you do) informs theory (what you think about what you do), and theory (what you think) informs practice (what you are doing). Theory and practice transform continuously into each other in a seamless flow.

So what does it take for your work to be seen as a possible contribution to new policy about what schools should be doing and how they should do it? What it takes is for you to show why your research should be taken seriously. This means producing a high-quality account that will command respect, and it brings us back to the purpose of this book. Here you get advice on how to do action research and how to present accounts of your research as quality theory, so that you will be seen as a top-notch theorist as well as an excellent practitioner.

Many people have already done this, including teachers who wish to improve practices in schools, and also teachers who never thought when they first began their action research that they would take it to Master's and PhD level. Examples are available here from teachers who show how they are engaging in the highest form of theory generation from within their classrooms. You can do this too, if you wish. There is nothing to stop you, provided you have the determination to do it. Our job is to help you get to where you want to be.

We return to these issues in Chapters 6 and 7. In the meantime, we address the practical issues of how to do action research, starting with what you need to think about before you begin, and then going on to talk about drawing up action plans and putting them into action.

CHAPTER 1

Thinking about what you need to do

This chapter deals with what you need to think about when planning an action research project in your workplace. The more time you can spend thinking in advance about the practicalities of your research, the better chance you have of a successful project. This chapter offers practical advice in terms of the kinds of questions you may ask, and possible ways of addressing them.

Thinking about what you need to do can be a valuable starting point. Because each person's situation is different, it is important to identify your own issues. A useful way is to draw up a list of 'Wh–?' questions:

- What?
- Who?
- Which?
- When?
- Where?
- Why?

These are reflective questions, and deal with immediate practical issues. They are often referred to as 'heuristic devices', that is, devices for finding out about something.

'Wh–?' into 'How do I . . .?' questions

'Wh–?' questions always have the capacity to turn into 'How do I . . .?' questions about practical action. 'How do I . . .?' signals your intent to take action towards improvement. For example:

Wh–? question	How do I . . .? questions
What is going on here?	*How* do I understand it?
	How do I improve it?

When you ask a 'Wh–?' question, always try to link it with the action research question, 'How do I . . .?' This will help you to keep your project practical, focused and manageable.

Here are some ideas to get you started.

What?

Here are two examples of 'What' into 'How do I . . .?' questions:

	What? questions	How do I . . .? questions
Example 1	What do I want to investigate?	How do I investigate it?
		How do I find out?
Example 2	What do I hope to achieve?	How do I achieve it?
		How do I manage the process?

Example 1
What do I want to investigate? How do I investigate it? How do I find out?

In action research you can investigate any and every aspect of your work. Aim to stay focused on only one aspect to begin with, otherwise the project may become too broad and get out of control. You may find that this aspect is symptomatic of, and embedded within, wider issues. Finding ways to stop one person bullying another in the classroom or staffroom may involve learning to negotiate with others. This may further involve learning about working with people.

Some researchers choose to address one issue first, as a first action reflection cycle, and then in later cycles go on to other issues as they emerge in a range of different ways.

Stay focused on your own practice. Don't worry about what needs to be improved elsewhere. Later you can relate your research to the rest of the school, but for now concentrate on what you are doing.

Example 2
What do I hope to achieve? How do I achieve it? How do I manage the process?

To begin with, stay focused on a short-term issue, such as 'What is the level of the children's achievement in English? How do I help them to improve their spelling?' It is important to bear in mind broader, longer-term questions such as 'How do I raise the level of achievement in the school?' or 'How do I encourage colleagues to develop more child-centred pedagogies?' because they give a vision of what you hope to achieve. The most practical place to begin is your immediate practice. This means keeping your eye on your vision as a guiding light and walking backwards from it, asking questions about what needs doing now, and how you can achieve it.

Here are some more examples of 'What?' into 'How do I . . .?' questions:

What? questions	How do I . . .? questions
What is the level of achievement in my maths class?	How do I improve my teaching of maths?
What do I need to do (or stop doing) as an educational leader?	How do I improve the quality of my educational leadership?
What is the focus of this lesson?	How do I stay on task?

Now draw up your own 'What?' into 'How do I . . .?' questions.

Who?

Here are two examples of 'Who?' into 'How do I . . .?' questions:

	Who? questions	How do I . . .? questions
Example 3	Who do I need to consult before doing my research?	How do I consult them? How do I negotiate to meet with them?
Example 4	Who will I involve?	How will I involve them? How will I negotiate this with them?

Example 3
Who do I need to consult? How do I consult them? How do I negotiate to meet with them?

Your action research includes a self-study of your own learning. You do not have to get anyone else's permission to study your own learning as you ask, research and answer questions of the kind, 'How do I improve what I am doing?' However, you must get permission to do your research from those whose learning you are intending to influence through your educational relationships, because you will involve them as sources of data or validation, and you have ethical and legal responsibilities to them. This means getting permissions in writing. You definitely need to consult your principal or manager, and possibly the Board of Governors (see McNiff *et al.* 2003: 49–57 for general advice on ethics in action research, and for examples of permissions letters and ethics statements). You must promise good ethical conduct, such as confidentiality and protection of people's anonymity for those who wish this, and their right to withdraw from the research. Robson (2002), McNamee and Bridges (2002) and Zeni (2001) contain useful guidance on ethical practices. You can also download the ethical guidelines of the British Educational Research Association from http://www.bera.ac.uk

When working with children and young people you must get written permission from their parents or legal caregivers. If you don't, you may find yourself dealing with litigation.

You must negotiate permission with colleagues and keep people informed, to avoid suggestions that your research is something mysterious. Be determinedly open about what you are doing and negotiate all round. Negotiating permission is part of the planning process. The more attention you pay at the planning stages, the greater your chances of success.

Sometimes ethical difficulties are encountered in action research when abuses of power are encountered. We are fortunate in the UK that academic freedom is protected under the law. Jack has addressed issues of power in relation to the growth of his educational knowledge in 'Action Research Expeditions: Do action researchers' expeditions carry hope for the future of humanity? How do we know? An enquiry into reconstructing educational theory and educating social formations' (Whitehead 2004b).

Example 4
Who will I involve? How do I involve others? How will I negotiate this with them?

Different people will be involved in your project in different ways, such as:

- research participants
- collaborative colleagues
- critical friends, validators and advisers
- interested observers.

Involving research participants

Who will you choose as participants to give you feedback on how you are getting on? A teacher might ask students whether he or she is helping them to learn. A principal may ask colleagues, 'What should I do to help you? What do you need from me? What do I need from you?'

Remember that participants are participants, not objects of study. You are asking questions about what you do, not about what they do, so they will give you feedback on how they respond to you. This feedback may support your claims to knowledge. If you say that you have improved your teaching of maths, your claim has to be supported by students' assessments of their own learning.

Involving collaborative colleagues

You may consider doing a collaborative action research project with other colleagues. You would ask questions such as:

- How do we improve our work?
- How do we raise the level of achievement of children in our classes?
- How do we ensure that the children in our school have access to special provision?

Doing action research collaboratively often involves individuals asking their 'How do I . . .?' questions and then inviting one another's responses to their provisional answers. The research becomes a matter of 'I's working together. Collaborative working can also involve individuals taking a collective stance towards a particular issue so that they become a 'we'. This can lead to powerful organisational learning and the development of a culture of enquiry (see Delong 2002).

Involving critical friends, validators and advisers

Other people can offer critical and constructive feedback – an essential part of evaluation. When you say, 'My work is better than it was before', you are making a big and important claim that needs to be backed up by strong evidence.

You would ask people for critical feedback throughout your research. These people would be sympathetic to what you are doing, but they must never agree with you just because they like you. Their feedback should help you to see things that you have not seen already, especially about your own and others' perceptions. Perhaps you were not aware that you talk more to girls than to boys. Perhaps you didn't see that your department is influenced by one particular voice. Critical friends can help you bring these issues to the surface.

Critical friends can also act as validators, that is, people who listen to or read your research reports. This would probably happen at specially convened validation meetings when you ask for more formal feedback on your work (see pages 94–5). They scrutinise your progress report and evidence, and give you feedback on whether you seem to be achieving your aims, or whether you need to rethink certain aspects.

Critical friends and validators can be drawn from your circle of professional colleagues. They can be other teachers, parents, students, managers, or people whose opinions you value. They should be able to offer critical insights that will help you develop your thinking and your practice.

Involving interested observers

Interested observers, that is, people who are interested but not directly involved in your research, may include parents, colleagues, governors and managers. They observe progress, and offer advice or comment when asked. It is important to keep them informed about progress. Aim to produce regular oral or written progress reports. You can ask for a few minutes at a staff meeting, or put a short report on the notice-board. By doing this you are not just keeping people informed – you are also setting an example of good professional practice.

Here are some more examples of 'Who?' into 'How do I . . .?' questions:

Who? questions	How do I . . .? questions
Who will read my research report?	How do I write for a particular audience?
Who will be my critical friends and validators?	How do I invite and negotiate with them?
Who will make judgements about the quality of my research?	How do I persuade them to listen to me and take my claims seriously?

Now draw up your own 'Who?' into 'How do I . . .?' questions.

Which?

Here are two examples of 'Which?' into 'How do I . . .?' questions.

	Which? questions	How do I . . .? questions
Example 5	Which issue shall I focus on for my research project?	How do I decide which aspects of my work to prioritise? How do I formulate a research question?
Example 6	Which people shall I choose to be research participants?	How do I select a group that will be representative of what I want to investigate? How do I perceive them in relation to me?

Example 5

Which issue shall I focus on for my research project? How do I decide which aspects of my work to prioritise? How do I formulate a research question?

You could choose many aspects of your work as a research topic. Beginning action researchers sometimes find it difficult to identify a topic and formulate a research question. So, to get started, think of something important to you, going on at this moment, that is related to your educational values and commitments; or think of something that is on your mind and won't go away. You may ask, at an individual level:

- As a class teacher, how do I stop bullying in my classroom? (Relating to your commitment to justice.)
- As a newly appointed head of department, how do I find ways of managing my role? (Relating to your commitment to good professional conduct.)
- As a principal, how do I manage my own process of self-evaluation? (Relating to your commitment to accountability.)

Or, at a collective level, you may ask:

- As a department, how do we draw up a policy for managing the curriculum? (Relating to your commitment to collaborative working.)
- As a group of post-holders, how do we draw up a school action plan? (Relating to your commitment to democratic ways of working.)
- As a committed staff, how do we create a culture of fairness throughout the school? (Relating to your commitment to compassion and kindness.)

Talking it through with other colleagues can be helpful, but it is up to you which aspects of your work you focus on.

You may be in a situation where you are required to do an action enquiry with a specific focus, especially if you are in a context where funding or arrangements for remitted time are linked with school policy. You may be asked to find ways of helping the school to raise its standards in numeracy or literacy. This is fine, but be careful not to encourage an expectation that you will succeed. Many stories are told about practitioners who linked their enquiries to specific outcomes and targets, and when the targets were not met the project was judged a failure. If you agree to undertake a project linked with identified outcomes, state clearly that your own and others' professional learning should be seen as a valuable outcome, not only modified behaviours. In debates about raising standards, which are usually about students achieving higher scores on tests, what is often not said is that the professional learning of teachers is a core factor in raising standards. What is also not often discussed is the issue of whose standards are important, and what they are standards of (see Chapter 6).

Throughout you need to be clear and confident about which issue you are researching, and why. If in doubt, talk with a colleague about why you came into teaching, and whether you are still enjoying your work as much as when you were a probationer. If you are, how can you explain why you are getting such a sense of fulfilment? If not, how can you change things so that you can regain your passion and commitment?

Example 6
Which people shall I choose to be research participants? How do I select a group that will be representative of what I want to investigate? How do I perceive them?

Although you ask, 'How do I improve what I am doing?', with the focus on yourself, your research is not isolationist. You are always in company with others, and your practice is always a social event. Even when you are on your own, you are never alone. At a personal level, you are always in networks of relationships. In your professional life, those relationships are to do with education, and are supported by educational values. When you ask how you can improve what you are doing, you imply that you are improving it for someone. This includes yourself, and the people for whom you have a responsibility. Therefore, to make judgements on whether or not you are practising in a way that is in someone else's interest, you have to get their feedback about whether they are benefiting.

This is key in selecting research participants. You are not doing research on them, or regarding them as data, as is usually the case in social science research where a researcher selects an experimental group. In experimental cases, the findings from studying one group can be generalised to other similar groups, and the experimental situation can be replicated. Instead, you are looking at how you are in relation with others, and you use their responses to you as evidence to support or question your claim to knowledge. If you are asking questions about how you can prevent bullying in your classroom, you may invite victims and bullies to say whether or not you are helping them to develop new kinds of relationships. If, as a group of post-holders, you are developing a whole-school plan, you would include others as participants, possibly the whole staff with some key individuals such as heads of department. It is up to you to decide who would be appropriate participants, in terms of both whether they are representative of the research issue and whether they can provide useful feedback.

Here are some more 'Which?' into 'How do I . . .?' questions:

Which? questions	How do I . . .? questions
Which teachers will be involved in the Citizenship programme?	How do I/we involve them?
Which children are designated for special support?	How do I/we support them?
Which parents do we urgently need to talk with?	How do we involve them more in their children's education?

Now draw up your own 'Which?' into 'How do I . . .?' questions.

When?

Here are two examples of 'When?' into 'How do I . . .?' questions:

	When? questions	How do I . . .? questions
Example 7	When will I do my action research?	How do I make time for it? How do I show the significance of my research?
Example 8	When will I make my work public?	How do I arrange for its dissemination? How do I get people to take my research seriously?

Example 7
When will I do my action research? How do I make time for it?
How do I show the significance of my research?

Action research is part of your everyday practice, something you do, not only something you read and write about. However, it is only a part, not the whole of your practice. Planning your research involves identifying and focusing fairly narrowly on a particular issue. As a language teacher you might want to improve your teaching of languages, but you cannot monitor all the work you do five days a week, so you would focus perhaps on one particular class. You could not monitor your work with every student in that class, so you would focus on just a few. You should decide which students will act as your research partici-pants, but you need to give reasons why you have chosen these and not others.

This has implications for how you explain the significance of your work. Traditional social science research tends to use the criteria of generalisability and replicability to assess the validity of the research and its findings. You are doing educational research, so you use differ-ent criteria and standards of judgement (see Chapter 5), because each situation is unique and needs to be judged in its own terms. You are aiming to transfer the understanding you have gained from studying one context to your wider practice. You might, for example, try out a technique that is successful in your research class(es) in other classes. When you tell people what you are doing, and show them your evidence, they may want to try it for themselves. You are inviting other people to learn with you. You are not imposing a model on them.

When do you make time for your research? This is a difficult issue. Although your research is part of your everyday practice, it does need time for planning, thinking, reading, gathering data and making sense of it in order to generate evidence, talking with critical friends, convening validation meetings, and writing a report. These are extra activities, and they need to be factored into your overall planning. If you are in one of the growing number of institutions that are taking workplace research seriously, you will be allocated remitted time. If you are one of the thousands of practitioners who do their research in addition to their normal work, you will have to make time. This means putting something out in order to bring your research in, and you need to make your own decisions about this. However you create this extra time, you have to factor it in.

Example 8
When will I make my work public? How do I arrange for its dissemination? How do I get people to take my work seriously?

Aim to set a time frame around your research and plan the different phases as much as possible. When do you begin and end? When do you complete your data gathering? When do you make your report available to others?

Making your work public is not only a matter of producing a report, although this is essential. It is also about getting people's feedback at regular intervals. You need to involve critical friends who will listen to your work in progress and offer advice about different aspects. Talking regularly with critical friends is important because they can keep you on track and also offer the moral support we all need when doing a special project. Contact with critical friends tends to be informal. A more formal exercise involves convening a validation group, which is a group of colleagues who you know will be supportive and will also offer critical feedback. This group meets at regular intervals, say, every six or ten weeks. They look at your evidence, offer their opinions on its quality, and listen to your provisional claims to knowledge. They give feedback, suggest direction, and perhaps request that you rethink your claims or produce stronger evidence. Validation meetings are seldom cosy. Your research must be seen by the wider community to have been subject to stringent critique, so that your claims are seen as valid. By engaging in such rigorous processes you are showing that you take your research seriously, and you expect others to do so too.

Here are some more examples of 'When?' into 'How do I . . .?' questions:

When? questions	How do I . . .? questions
When will I begin gathering data, and when will I finish?	How do I understand my research as a bounded project?
When will I involve participants?	How do I decide who to ask, and for what purpose?
When will I do my reflecting and writing?	How do I negotiate with my family that I need study time and they have to do the cooking instead of me?

Now draw up your own 'When' into 'How do I . . .?' questions.

Where?

Here are two examples of 'Where?' into 'How do I . . .?' questions:

	Where? questions	'How do I . . .?' questions
Example 9	Where do I find my resources?	How do I ensure that I have all the resources I need? How do I get them?
Example 10	Where will I study?	How do I find quiet spaces in my busy life? How do I make time and space for reflection?

Example 9
Where do I find my resources? How will I ensure that I have all the resources I need? How do I get them?

You will need resources in the form of people, time and materials.

People
We said on pages 10–11 that the following groups of people will be involved in your research:

Research participants. These will be drawn from the people you are working with directly, such as your students or colleagues. Advice is given on pages 62–3 about which participants to select. You must get permission from your participants, or their advocates, to involve them, and you must observe all ethical practices in relation to them (pages 34–5).

Critical friends and validators. These will be drawn from your professional circle. Always ensure you invite their involvement, and never take them for granted. Be sure to thank them after each meeting, and perhaps also send them a thank-you note afterwards. These are some of your best allies, so nurture them.

Interested and supportive observers. These people are not directly involved in your research, but they offer good will and advice when needed. Again, never take them for granted. They don't have to be there, so let them know how much their support is appreciated.

It is your responsibility to approach all these people and invite their involvement. The practical issues you need to think about in advance are about how and when you should approach them, how you will frame your questions, and what you need to do to secure their support.

Time

Sometimes it is possible to negotiate study time or even study leave. Check with your head of department or professional manager whether this may be the case, or make an appointment to discuss it with your principal. Do not expect time to be given. If it is, regard it as a bonus and be grateful. Most practitioners simply do not get any time considerations for their research. Be aware of this from the beginning, and don't complain later.

Materials

You will need practical resources such as stationery and photocopying facilities. Check in advance what you might need, and ensure that you know who to ask. Will you be able to draw on the department budget? Will you be able to use the school's video camera? It is useful to draw up a list of materials in advance, as well as ideas on how you can get them. Don't leave it until your project is under way, otherwise you may experience serious interruptions if, say, a tape recorder is not available or you cannot photocopy a critical worksheet.

Example 10
Where will I study? How do I find quiet spaces in my busy life?
How do I make time and space for reflection?

Doing an action research project involves study time. This may not be much, but you still need to cater for a certain amount of reading, reflection and writing. Finding a space to study can be problematic.

It is helpful, but not always possible, to have a room of your own, where you can leave things ready for next time. Most people have to share their space with others and also share resources such as the family computer, which can sometimes present difficulties, but you should stake your claim as much as anyone else. You have a right to study.

Given that you may not have much access to private space, try to find ways of fitting in study time whenever and wherever you can. Here are some ideas.

Reading

Reading can be time-consuming, so fit it in at every opportunity. Carry a book with you. You can do a lot of reading on a ten-minute bus ride. Reading is important because it can help you to contextualise your research within bigger issues, and it can also spark off ideas in your mind. Try to get into the habit of reading instead of watching television when you don't really want to see the programme, but balance this out with the need for recreation and relaxation. Just be aware of your choices. Time spent looking out of windows can be marvellously restorative.

Reflecting

When we are involved in something, we often don't make sense of it while we are actually doing it. We just do it because our feelings and experience tell us it is right. When we get a quiet space, away from the action, it begins to make sense. Those quiet spaces can be difficult to come by, given the busy and pressured lives that most teachers lead. They can, however, be found, although they often have to be created. One deputy head teacher, now studying for her doctorate with Jack, was despondent over her lack of time. Discovering that she made a 40-minute car journey to and from work, Jack suggested she talk into a hands-free tape recorder and review the day on the way home. It worked! Perhaps you could fit in a short walk after work each day for reflection, or do the gardening for a while. Sit and look out of the window. Many of us feel guilty when we take time out, but it is really important to find time to consolidate and feel grounded.

If you can't get time and space to yourself, try to think in an active way while you are doing the shopping or the housework. You can structure your thinking by asking focused questions such as, 'What did I do from 9 a.m. to 11 a.m.? What did I do well? What might I have done better? How would I do things differently next time? What have I learned from the experience?' Avoid turning reflection into a time for beating yourself up or negative thinking, which we all tend to do, especially when working in difficult circumstances. Rather than dwell on a negative experience, accept that it happened and then think of ways in which you can turn it into a positive one. So the children were badly behaved. What can you do tomorrow to capture their attention?

Writing

Writing can take several forms, such as journal keeping, writing progress reports and writing the final report. You can write in straight text or use a multimedia format.

Keeping a journal can be useful and can help you reflect on your work. Detailed advice will be given on journal writing in Chapter 4. It helps if you keep your journal regularly. Aim to write it up every two or three days, and use it to record your reflections and learnings as well as your activities. Writing up a journal is often easier than writing a report, because you can do it at odd times and anywhere you have space to write.

Writing progress and final reports is not fitted so easily into odd spaces. They are important documents that keep you and everyone else up to date. You just need to find a quiet space on your own to write. Marian Nugent, now an assistant principal in a Dublin post-primary school (see her Master's dissertation, Nugent 2000, on www.jeanmcniff.com), got up regularly at 5.30 a.m. for two years to fit in study time and writing before she went to work. If you seriously want a degree or certificate you simply have to find time and space for it. You are not alone. Thousands of teachers like you are putting study time into their already crowded lives, much to the benefit of their students and the teaching profession.

Here are some more examples of 'Where?' into 'How do I . . .?' questions:

'Where?' questions	'How do I . . .?' questions
Where do we put the computers in school?	How do we ensure that all children have access to limited resources?
Where do children go when they need help?	How do we ensure that children know what supports are available to them?
Where do teaching staff meet during their break times?	How do I ensure that the staff room is welcoming and conducive to collegial talk?

Now draw up your own 'Where?' into 'How do I . . .?' questions.

Why?

Here are two examples of 'Why?' into 'How do I . . .?' questions:

	Why? questions	How do I . . .? questions
Example 11	Why should I choose this piece of data?	How do I integrate it into my other data? How do I show its relevance?
Example 12	Why do I want to pursue this particular research issue?	How do I understand myself as a living contradiction? How do I manage the tension?

Example 11
Why should I choose this piece of data? How do I integrate it into my other data? How do I show its relevance?

Chapter 5 explains what kind of data you should aim to gather and how you can do this. Broadly speaking, you should aim to gather data that is relevant and meaningful to your research question. If your research question is to do with how you can help students to improve their reading skills, you should gather data to show what their reading skills were like at the beginning of your project, and how they may have improved (or not) throughout the course of your project. You can use quantitative data, such as test scores, as well as qualitative data, such as interviews, conversations, letters and memos.

In projects like this it is important to remember that your research is about what you are doing and your potential influence in the learning of others. So, although you are aiming to help your students to improve their reading skills, the research focus is on how you are helping them and what you are learning from the process. The data you gather about your students' progress has to be seen in relation to what you are doing to influence their learning. Teaching and learning in this case are in a symbiotic relationship. It is also important to remember that this is a relationship of influence, not one of cause and effect. You cannot say that you are causing their achievement or lack of it, but you can say that you believe you are influencing their learning. The data you gather should be relevant to this claim that you are influencing their learning.

It is up to you what kinds of data you gather, but make sure that all your data are relevant to the question. Also aim to gather several kinds of data, for example test scores, interviews, letters and memos. The more relevant data you gather, the more you will have to select from when you come to generating evidence.

Example 12
Why do I want to pursue this particular research issue? How do I understand myself as a living contradiction? How do I manage the tension?

Chapter 2 explains how many people take as a starting point for their research their experience of holding certain values that are denied in their practice. For example, you may believe in good timekeeping as a mark of a purposeful attitude to study, but you find that the Traveller children you work with do not always prioritise punctuality or regular attendance. Or perhaps recently you have been sleeping rather poorly and have arrived late at school on two occasions. Perhaps good timekeeping is important for you in theory but in practice it is not working. In this case you could say that you are experiencing yourself as a living contradiction (Whitehead 1989). How do you manage the tension?

Some people undertake their action enquiries with a view to solving what they perceive to be a problem, but it is equally acceptable to approach an issue as something to be managed and lived with, rather than solved. Many issues in life defy solutions and, in many instances, a solution is not the aim. You would not wish to interfere with Traveller culture, for example, but it is your responsibility as the Traveller resource teacher to find ways of bringing together traditional school expectations around punctuality and regular attendance with the expectations of minority cultures. It can be helpful to see dilemmas not as problems to be solved so much as a matter of arranging a harmonious relationship between divergent forms of living. How you manage your sleep patterns is for you to decide. Perhaps part of your action enquiry could be introducing meditation into your lessons, from which you may benefit as much as your students. Action research goes well beyond classroom walls and other artificial boundaries.

Here are some more examples of 'Why?' into 'How do I . . .?' questions:

Why? questions	How do I . . .? questions
Why is it important to ensure good ethical conduct?	How do I ensure good ethical conduct?
Why am I doing this?	How do I offer explanations for my practice?
Why don't they understand what I am getting at?	How do I communicate more effectively?

Now draw up your own 'Why?' into 'How do I . . .?' questions.

How?

Asking 'How do I . . .?' questions signals your intent to take action towards improvement. It can be helpful to develop your first 'How do I . . .?' question into more specific or more extended 'How do I . . .?' questions. This can be seen as a form of progressive focusing (Parlett and Hamilton 1977) that can help you to refine your planning and keep your project focused and manageable. Here are some examples:

	'How do I . . .?' questions	Extended 'How do I . . .?' questions
Example 13	How do I generate evidence?	How do I produce evidence and not simply illustrations of practice? How do I articulate my standards of judgement and practice?
Example 14	How do I disseminate my work?	How will I produce a high-quality text? How will I disseminate it?

Example 13
How do I generate evidence? How do I produce evidence and not simply illustrations of practice? How do I articulate my standards of judgement and practice?

Chapter 5 explains how to generate evidence from the data in relation to specifically articulated criteria and standards of judgement.

The generation of evidence is vital in action research. Also vital is understanding what evidence looks like and, especially, how evidence is different from illustration. Imagine, for example, that your project is around how using visual, auditory and kinaesthetic (VAK) approaches may help your students to improve their learning of maths. You gather data in the form of videotapes as your students use VAK approaches during maths lessons, and you also gather pieces of their artwork and poetry about their experience of studying maths. When you write your report you insert stills from your videos and the pieces of artwork and poetry. It is essential, however, not to present these pieces of work simply as illustrations. If you did, your reader would rightly ask, 'So what? These are nice examples and illustrations, but what is their significance? What am I supposed to gather from them?' For examples of practice to stand as evidence, they have to show their relationship to the research issue. If your study is to demonstrate how you believe your encouragement of students to use VAK approaches is helping them to improve their learning in maths, you need to spell out the connections between what you hoped to achieve in your research and whether you believe it is being achieved. Perhaps a piece of artwork shows how a student is able to make symbolic connections between numbers. Perhaps a piece of poetry expresses a child's delight at manipulating figures successfully. You would suggest that the examples of practice are instances of how you feel you are achieving your research goals; and, because your goals can also be understood as a living out of your values, you could say that your values are the living standards by which you judge your practice.

Understanding one's values as one's living standards of practice and judgement is a powerful stance. You can show how you undertook your project in order to try to live your educational values in your practice, and you can show how you are meeting your own high standards through the production of validated evidence.

Example 14
How do I disseminate my work? How will I produce a high-quality text? How will I disseminate it?

We are making the point throughout that your action research has the potential to influence future policy, which itself has the potential to influence the life choices of yourself and other teachers. The key is in the quality of the research and also in the quality of the text.

Action research accounts must be of a quality that will withstand public scrutiny and challenge. Accounts need to be subjected to public critique and testing, in order to avoid challenges of poor-quality research and to establish the validity of the claims contained in the report and the processes by which those claims have been arrived at.

This high-quality research then has to be presented as an equally high-quality text. Like it or not, people's work is judged in terms of the texts they produce as much as in terms of the work itself. The word 'text' means not only a written manuscript but also other forms of representation such as film, video or storytelling. When we present our work we are representing the experience of doing the work, and we are judged on both counts.

Chapter 6 gives advice on how to produce a quality research report. Here we are making the case that you have to be aware of the need to produce texts, and to cater for this from the beginning of your project. This means keeping careful records continuously, and also getting into the habit of writing up.

Producing a text is intense, time-consuming work. It can be most frustrating when ideas do not hang together, or when sentences slip away like jelly. Even the most experienced writers will tell you how much they struggle with creating a text. However, there is nothing quite like he thrill experienced when it does come right and you see what was a vague idea emerge as a coherent and well-disciplined argument. This all takes effort and commitment, but there is a lot at stake and a lot worth struggling for.

Now, over time, systematically transform all your 'How do I . . .?' questions into more refined and operational 'How do I . . .?' questions. The more you can do this, the more you can give yourself practical prompts and guidelines that will help you stay on task and keep the whole project in perspective.

SUMMARY

This chapter has given advice on what you need to think about before you begin your project. Time spent on planning is time well spent. The better it is planned, the more chance your project has of success. Turning practical 'Wh-?' questions into 'How do I . . .?' questions can help you to register your intent to take action towards improvement.

You will have ideas of your own that are not mentioned in this chapter. Asking heuristic questions can be a useful way into planning, but you may have other strategies. We urge you to be as creative as you like in thinking about what you need to do. It is your project, and it should be an exciting and enjoyable time. Try to leave as little as possible to chance. If it does all fall apart, as sometimes happens, you will know that you did your best, and you will already have resources in place to begin anew. If it all goes according to plan, you will have reason to congratulate yourself on forward planning and ensuring the best quality of life for yourself and others.

The next chapter is also about planning, and gives advice about drawing up action plans.

CHAPTER 2

Drawing up action plans

Teachers are often required to draw up action plans for their work. This chapter gives advice about drawing up action plans for your research project, but the ideas may just as easily be used for drawing up an action plan for, say, how a school can engage in whole-school evaluation, or how post-holders can get a better understanding of their organisational responsibilities or manage their role.

An action plan communicates the idea that a project or task should be undertaken in a systematic way. There is a notional goal, and the idea is to achieve the goal via a series of systematic steps. In action research, the aim is to take action in order to improve something, usually practice.

It is generally believed that, if the action plan is followed, then an improved end state can be achieved. This is not always the case. Sometimes it is, but often things do not go according to plan, because we are all free and unpredictable humans and do not always do as expected. Unfortunately, many people believe that action research is a matter of rolling out a designed plan and all will be well, so when things go wrong, as they sometimes do, people tend to think that the practitioner-researcher is at fault rather than question their own assumptions about neat human processes and the wish for the security of closure.

There are many action plans in the literature of action research that offer action steps (see McNiff and Whitehead 2002: 39–58 for an overview). The approach developed by Jack Whitehead (1989, 2004a) forms the conceptual basis of this book. This approach invites practitioner-researchers to ask themselves questions about their work (see page 29). These questions are organised in a coherent sequence so, in those cases when the action does go according to plan, the answers form a straightforward story of the research and what you learned, and can then be written up as a report. In those cases when things do not go according to plan, the research story tells what happened and how you learned from the experience. Such stories can be rich sources of deep learning (see the example on page 41).

Remember that an action plan is a plan, not the reality, and acts only as a map, not a set of directives. No one is forced to follow someone else's map. You may if you wish, or you can design your own map. The main thing is to get to where you hope to be, and to be able to articulate the route you took and say why you went that way.

Action planning means planning for several things:

1   Planning to take action and monitor the action in the social world
2   Planning to reflect and to monitor your learning
3   Planning to keep records of action and learning
4   Planning to involve others.

These points are the focus of the sections in this chapter. Three examples of action plans appear at the end of the chapter. Detailed advice about implementing your action plans is given in Chapter 3.

1 PLANNING TO TAKE ACTION AND MONITOR THE ACTION IN THE SOCIAL WORLD

To note: Action is usually understood and written about as action in the social world. Thinking and learning are actions too, of a different kind. The actions in your mind (what you think) are interrelated with your actions in the world (what you do). A distinction is made in this chapter for analytical purposes, but in reality the two are inseparable.

Planning to take action in the social world

When drawing up your action plan, think about why you are doing your research and what you hope to achieve. This is especially important in self-study, where the focus is on studying one's own practice.

Practice is assumed to be value-laden and value-driven. Practice is different from action. You can laugh, for example, or trip over, which are actions but not practice. Practice is always purposeful and therefore value-laden.

We all hold different values, which we learn from our different cultures. Cruel actions are value-driven in the same way as kind ones are. It is up to each person to choose which values they live by.

Jack Whitehead sees the basis of an action plan in the idea that throughout our lives we try to realise our values in our practices. As teachers, we try to realise our educational values in practice. These values come to act as our guiding principles. Often, however, we find ourselves in situations where it is impossible to realise our values, or even to live in the direction of our values. In this case, says Jack (Whitehead 1989), we experience ourselves as living contradictions, because we hold values that are systematically denied in practice. This may be because we ourselves are denying our own values, or because other people are doing so and preventing us from living as we would like to. For example, a teacher may believe that children should speak for themselves but, when watching a videotape of herself, comes to see that she does most of the talking. She tends to ask questions and then answer them herself, rather than offer the children the opportunity of learning in their own way. Another teacher believes in fairness for all, and yet when his children's capacities are judged in terms of a specific and limited set of skills, he does little to champion the children's rights to learn in their own way. Many teachers find themselves in social and organisational situations where their educational values around the freedom and creativity of people, especially children, are systematically denied.

A strong basis for drawing up an action plan, according to Jack, is to come to understand the degree to which we may be experiencing ourselves as a living contradiction, and to find ways of resolving the tension so that we can live in a way that does no violence to our own or others' integrity. He has organised these ideas as follows:

- I experience a concern when some of my educational values are denied in my practice;
- I imagine a solution to that concern;
- I act in the direction of the imagined solution;
- I evaluate the outcome of the solution;
- I modify my practice, plans and ideas in the light of the evaluation.

(Whitehead 1989, 2004a)

These ideas emerged from a collaborative research project working with six teachers over 1975–6 to improve the learning of 11–14-year-olds (Whitehead 1976). You can access the original report at http://www.bath.ac.uk/~edsajw/writings/ilmagall.pdf

The ideas can then transform into an understanding of what action research involves:

- We review our current practice;
- identify an aspect that we want to improve;
- imagine a way forward;
- try it out;
- and take stock of what happens.
- We modify our plan in the light of what we have found, and continue with the 'action';
- evaluate the modified action;
- and reconsider the position in the light of the evaluation.

(McNiff et al. 2003: 58)

This set of steps can in turn transform into a series of questions that anyone can ask themselves about any aspect of their work. It is also possible to show how these questions are related to one's values base.

- What is my concern?
- Why am I concerned?
- What kind of evidence do I produce to show why I am concerned?
- What can I do about it?
- What will I do about it?
- What kind of evidence do I produce to show that what I am doing is having an influence?
- How do I evaluate that influence?
- How do I ensure that any judgements I make are reasonably fair and accurate?
- How do I modify my practice in the light of my evaluation?

This is a generic action plan, which can be modified to suit your own circumstances.

Planning to monitor your action in the social world

As well as planning to take action, you also need to plan how you are going to keep track of what you do. You need to decide who will monitor, what will be monitored, and how it will be monitored.

Who will monitor?

Will you monitor yourself, or ask someone else? Will you ask your students or a colleague to observe you in action? Will you keep a journal? Will it be a traditional written one, or an audio or video journal?

What will be monitored?

Whose practice will you monitor, yours or your students', or both? How will you keep records of what you are doing, and also of how your students are responding to you? Will you focus on one aspect of your work, or several?

How will it be monitored?

What kinds of record will you keep? Field notes, observations, record sheets? Will you develop your own portfolio, and invite your students to do the same? Will you gather quantitative or qualitative data, or both kinds? Why? How will you incorporate quantitative data into your self-study?

These issues and others are developed in Chapter 5.

2 PLANNING TO REFLECT AND MONITOR YOUR LEARNING

By undertaking your research project you are already showing that you are open to new learning. Like many researchers, you will probably find that you learn not only about substantive issues such as subject matters but also about your own capacity for new learning. By undertaking an action research project you are taking action in two domains. The first is action in the world – the social world 'out there' (as explained in the previous section). Equally important, however, is the action you take in your personal world of learning – the mental world 'in here'. What is going on 'in here' influences greatly what goes on 'out there'. It is just as important, therefore, to plan for how you are going to keep track of your reflections and evaluations with regard to your personal learning as well as of your social action.

This can best be done by keeping a reflective journal, where you ask questions about your learning in relation to what you are doing (see Chapter 4). These questions can take the forms:

- What have I done?
- What have I learned?
- What is the significance of my learning?

- How do I modify my practice in the light of my evaluation (see below)?

You need to keep careful records of your learning to show how it is developing from within your practice and feeding back into your practice.

Some researchers choose their learning as the focus of their enquiry (see the examples on pages 38 and 71).

If you wanted to take your learning as your focus, you could use the same generic action plan, asking questions about what you already know and what you need to learn. Your questions could look something like this:

- What is my concern (about what I know)? What do I need to learn?
- Why am I concerned (about what I know)? Why is this an important issue for me?
- What kind of evidence do I produce to show my concern (about what I know and what I need to learn)?
- What can I do about it (about what I know)? How do I critique what I know? How am I going to learn more?
- What will I do about it?
- What kind of evidence do I produce to show the potential influence of my learning?
- How do I ensure that any judgements I make about my learning and the learning of others are reasonably fair and accurate?
- How do I modify my practice in the light of my new learning? How do my practice and my learning develop together?

If you wished, you could map your social action plan onto your learning action plan. This would give you the following overall action plan:

- What is my concern (about what I do and what I know)?
- Why am I concerned (about what I do and what I know)?
- How do I show the situation as it is, and why I am concerned (both about what I do and what I know)?
- What can I do about what I do and what I know?
- What will I do?
- What kind of evidence do I produce to show that what I am doing in the one domain is influencing the other?
- How do I evaluate that influence?

- How do I ensure that any judgements I make are reasonably fair and accurate?
- How do I modify my practice in one domain in the light of my evaluation in the other?

You could also focus on your action as one cycle and then focus on learning as another.

By foregrounding the importance of learning as much as action, you come to the point where you are evaluating not only what you are doing in terms of social action but also what you are thinking in terms of learning. Your learning can be understood in relation to what you believed when you first undertook your project, how you learned about your own beliefs and began to critique them by taking social action, how you came to modify your practice (in both domains) in the light of your new learning, and how your new learning is in turn feeding back into new practice. You are therefore generating new practices (what you do) and new knowledge (what you have come to know about what you do). Your learning becomes a form of metacognition about your action (McDonagh 2004).

This aspect of focusing on and evaluating your own learning, as well as taking stock of and evaluating social practice, is often overlooked in the literature. We authors, Jean (McNiff 1989) and Jack (Whitehead 1976), have consistently made it explicit in our own writings, and we are delighted with the upsurge of interest in focusing on learning in practitioner action research. It is a vital aspect if practice is to be understood as praxis, that is, informed, morally committed action, and not just activity.

How to keep records of practice and of learning is dealt with in the next chapter.

3 PLANNING TO KEEP RECORDS OF ACTION AND LEARNING

To show the systematic nature of your enquiry as you investigate your actions and your learning, you need to monitor it closely. This means deciding how you are going to keep records on a systematic basis. The records you keep will act as stores for the data you gather. You will in turn transform this data into evidence (see Chapter 5). At this point you need to think about two issues:

- How are you going to keep records of your action?
- How are you going to keep records of your reflection and learning?

Keeping records of action

This is usually done by using written documents or live methods.

Written methods include:
- Personal field notes
- Personal logs and diaries
- Questionnaires
- Surveys
- Record sheets.

Live methods include:
- Interviews
- Role play
- Action recorded on audio or videotape.

Keeping records of reflection and learning

This is usually done by keeping a research diary or journal, and using that as a means of showing how the learning has developed. Research journals can be in written form, or in audio and videotape recorded form. You can also monitor your learning by keeping files of correspondence with other people, in which you talk about how your learning is developing. By keeping these kinds of systematic records you can track how your learning is developing and influencing your practice. You may find instances of how your new behaviours demonstrate changed attitudes, which are the outcomes of new learning.

Further advice is given in Chapter 3.

4 PLANNING TO INVOLVE OTHERS

Doing your action research always involves other people. As noted throughout, although your research is about 'I' if you are working individually, or 'we' if you are working collectively, your research inevitably influences others in some way. You need to ensure, therefore, that you have permission and authorisation to do the research, and you also need to have the good will of others. You can secure this good will by demonstrating good faith yourself, especially by showing care for ethical considerations.

The ethics of involving others

We have emphasised the importance of paying attention to ethical considerations in action research (page 18). Your ethical principles often provide
the explanatory framework for why you are doing what you are doing. You
do not need anyone's permission to engage in a self-study of your own
learning, but if the learning of others is part of your research, then you
must get ethical clearance before you begin, especially as this relates to
involving other people as participants and potential sources of data.

Issues of ethics fall into three broad categories:

- Negotiating access
- Protecting your participants
- Assuring good faith.

Negotiating access

At an organisational level, this means that you have to ask your manager or
principal if you may do your research as it relates to the learning of others.
They in turn may have to negotiate your request with people in positions
senior to them, such as boards of management. You must get permission
in writing. Examples of letters of permission are available in McNiff *et al.*
(2003: 53–7). If permission is denied there is little you can do. Usually,
however, managers are only too pleased to grant permission, especially if
your project appears to be valuable to the organisation. If your project is
about how you believe you can improve students' performance in maths,
you will probably get overwhelming support. As we said on page 13, take
care, in instances like this, that you don't set up an expectation that you will
definitely improve students' performance, in which case the credibility of
your research would be tied to improved student performance. Some writers in action research do unfortunately make this strong behavioural link,
and encourage practitioners to set clear targets that they hope to achieve
through their action research. Others, including us (Jack and Jean), take the
view that your professional learning is every bit as valuable an outcome as
students' performance, on the basis that you must take responsibility for
your own teaching but you cannot take responsibility for your students'
learning. Provided you can show that you have improved your own practice
as a teacher in relation to your students' learning, that is enough. What your
students do is up to them. This point does emphasise the need to be clear
about what you are hoping to achieve, to keep your expectations in perspective, and to have goals in relation to what you can achieve for yourself.

Negotiating access and obtaining permission to do your research are important in relation to all participants, and essential when you are working with children. You must seek and obtain written permission from any participant to involve them in your research. In the case of children and vulnerable people, you must seek and obtain written permission from parents and caregivers. This is no longer only a matter of professional courtesy but also potentially a matter of legality. If it were discovered that you had involved children in your research without appropriate permissions, it could cost you dearly.

Protecting your participants

Protecting your participants means that you must place their welfare above your own at all times. This means promising confidentiality and anonymity if they want this. When you produce your reports, never mention a person's or an organisation's name unless you have their written permission to do so. In the case of people, give them numbers or initials. In the case of organisations, give them a fictitious name, but take care that the name might not already belong to a real organisation. Often participants wish to be named, and this should also be respected.

If you promise confidentiality, you must keep your promise. We all know that if one person shares a secret with another, they are already potentially sharing the secret with the world.

If people decide that they no longer wish to be involved in your research, you must grant them their right to withdraw, and also promise that all data about them will be destroyed.

To safeguard all these points, draw up ethics statements and distribute them to all participants (see McNiff *et al.* 2003: 53–4 for examples of ethics statements). This is not just a methodological nicety. It is part of good research practice and goes some way to ensuring your own credibility. Remember that credibility is like dry ice (Shulman 2002, cited in Joan Whitehead and Bernie Fitzgerald 2004a), which thaws at the temperatures required for human living. Once thawed, it cannot be refrozen. Credibility has to be protected and maintained, because once it goes, it seldom comes back.

Assuring good faith

Let people know that you are to be trusted. Build a reputation for good practice and personal integrity. This means keeping your promises, demonstrating courtesy and respect to others at all times, and never asking someone to do something that you are not prepared first to do yourself.

You will get good responses from people when they trust you. If they do not feel their trust is rightly placed, the quality of your research will suffer.

Most importantly, let people know that you are enjoying the experience of learning with and from them. Let them know that you have more to learn from them than they do from you. You have work to do, and it can be done better together than alone. Once you have put all measures in place to ensure good ethical practice, go for it, and do a research project that will contribute to people's learning far beyond your own context and realise your potential for influencing the future.

SUMMARY

This chapter has outlined what you need to think about in drawing up an action plan and deciding how to monitor the action, both in terms of social action and also in terms of learning. Chapter 3 gives advice about how to put these plans into action. Three case stories then follow that show how people did this in different contexts.

Before that, here are three examples of action plans.

Examples of action plans

Here are three examples of action plans that work in terms of social action and in terms of learning.

Example 1
How do I encourage trusting staff relationships?

My context
I am a newly appointed head teacher in a school that has experienced some internal dissent in recent times. Staff relations are known to be tense. I need to draw up an action plan for my first week at work. What do I need to address immediately?

What is my concern?
My concern is that there is a history of poor relationships among teaching staff, and lack of trust between staff and senior management. I need to get these relationships right in order to develop high-quality academic work.

Why am I concerned?
My previous experience tells me that a school cannot go forward successfully with internal divisions. Quality of learning is grounded in trusting

and caring relationships. Staff have to feel good about themselves if they are to feel good about their work and their students.

What kind of evidence do I produce to show why I am concerned?
On the first day I will call a staff meeting. As part of the agenda I will raise the issue of the need for good relationships, and I will register my intent to give priority to building a good working atmosphere throughout the school and invite everyone's cooperation and good will. I will let staff know that during my first week I hope to talk personally with every one of them. I will tell them that I am approaching this task as my personal research programme, and I will make clear that I will not actively record those meetings because I want them to be as comfortable as possible with a view to building trust. I will write my impressions in my journal, and also write up my field notes in my research diary, and later extract from the data some key points that I may use as evidence.

What can I do about the situation?
Several courses of action are immediately evident. I can:

● meet with every member of staff

● meet with senior and middle managers and invite them to come up with ideas on how to improve staff relations

● invite all members of staff to a 'bonding' weekend – no, far too early for that

● make available a 'suggestions' box? – probably not a good idea

● ask my daughter for her ideas – she is imaginative and good at relationships

● write down other ideas as they come to me.

What will I do about it?
Individual meetings are enough for the first week. I will go slowly and just try to establish the fact that we can have friendly and professional conversations with one another.

What kind of evidence will I produce to show that what I am doing is having an influence?
At the end of the week I will invite all members of staff to write down their impressions on whether my strategy is making any difference in establishing a good working atmosphere. I will say this at the morning staff meeting,

and make it clear that people can submit their comments anonymously, in envelopes that I will provide, and on a voluntary basis. I will invite them to take the weekend to think about it, and let me have their comments by the following Tuesday 9 a.m. I will put all responses in my data archive, ready to select some later that show depth of feeling as evidence of whether or not I am succeeding in developing trusting relationships.

How do I evaluate my influence?

I will look for indications in the letters that suggest a movement towards improved relationships and reduction in hostilities. If the data show that this is the case, I will take it as a sign that my strategy is working, even if in a small way.

How do I ensure that any judgements I make are reasonably fair and accurate?

I will ask the three members of the senior management team to act as a short-term validation group. In week two I will share with them my provisional findings and ask them to confirm whether, as established members of staff, they feel I am right to believe that my strategy is working.

How do I modify my practice in the light of my evaluation?

- I will continue to arrange to meet with every member of staff on a regular basis.
- I will invite members of staff to become participants in my research programme, strictly on a voluntary basis.
- I will put out a small questionnaire asking:
  - What are we doing well?
  - What could we do better?
  - What should we do differently?
- Responses are to be anonymous, returned by the end of week three in envelopes provided by me.
- I will invite staff to appoint a committee to plan with me a calendar of social events together.
- I will begin writing up my own progress report, ready to disseminate to staff by the end of week five.

Example 2 How do I learn about 'difference' and 'the other'?

My context

I am coordinator of the Personal, Social and Health Education programme in our school, and have also been asked to coordinate our new Citizenship

Education programme. I have just heard that I have been invited to go on a two-week exchange with a teacher in South Africa as part of my professional preparation for the job. I am thrilled at the opportunity but am also rather apprehensive.

What is my concern?

I am not confident around my subject matters. I do not feel I have enough knowledge about the issues to coordinate the Citizenship Education programme and provide leadership in developing curricula and appropriate pedagogies or materials. The idea of two weeks in South Africa is marvellous, but I know that social tensions still exist and again I am anxious that I don't know enough about the issues. I am also concerned that all I have to go on are my own assumptions about the issues, and these may be inappropriate or even incorrect.

Why am I concerned?

I am worried that my lack of knowledge will continue to eat away at my confidence, and also that it will jeopardise both the visit and also later development of our school programmes. I am most concerned that I will do or say something inappropriate in South Africa and possibly offend my hosts. I have strong feelings about justice and equality. I don't know how these values are lived out in South Africa, or what current attitudes are. I don't seem to know much!

What kind of evidence do I produce to show why I am concerned?

I will regard the visit as a research project. I will write down my reflections in my research journal. I will write to some trusted colleagues, sharing my misgivings. I will begin to keep a video diary of my thoughts and impressions. Later I can extract evidence from these data to show my apprehensions about my current state of knowledge.

What can I do about it?

- I can share my anxieties with my hosts before I get there. Is this a good idea? I don't know them and they may be offended by my questions.
- I can do some reading around South African social and political issues (where do I find time? – another research project!).
- I can do some reading around issues of 'difference' and 'otherness', as well as around justice and equality. Where do I access these literatures? I'll ask our school librarian.

- I can write down my own thoughts about difference, 'otherness', justice and equality. More data!
- I can adopt a 'wait-and-see' attitude, while maintaining an open mind and respectful attitude.

What will I do?

I will aim to do all of the above. When I get to South Africa I will listen carefully and aim to monitor my learning both about the issues and also about how I am learning.

What kind of evidence do I produce to show that what I am doing is having an influence?

I will keep regular records of my own learning. This will be crucial when I later come to look for data to show how my knowledge is developing. My records will take the form of my personal reflective journal, emails of experiences to family, friends and colleagues, and photos of me in action with colleagues in South Africa. I may find other ways when I am there.

How do I evaluate my influence?

I am aiming to understand my own learning, and how it influences my actions. I will specifically gather data about what I am learning and how this is enabling me to act with justice and respect for all. Later I will take from the data specific instances of when this happened. These instances can act as pieces of evidence that may show whether I am living according to my democratic values.

How do I ensure that any judgements I make are reasonably fair and accurate?

I hope to find some colleagues in South Africa with whom I can talk about my lack of knowledge of the issues and my willingness to learn. I hope they will be willing to help me monitor what I am learning and whether my attitudes need to change and are possibly changing. Before I go I will ask three members of my team to act as critical friends throughout, and on my return I will ask them to comment on what I have learned and on my own perceptions of my processes of learning.

How do I modify my practice in the light of my evaluation?

I hope that my learning will help me to gain confidence in providing leadership for my team as we develop our Citizenship Education programme. I hope I will communicate any new learning to them, and inspire them also to critique and modify their knowledge around the issues and check out their own assumptions.

Example 3
How do I learn from failure?

My context

I have just brought to a premature close an action research project that did not work out. I wanted to investigate whether I could encourage children to think critically, because I believe children should learn to challenge their own and other people's assumptions. Now other members of staff have complained to me and the principal that my children are talking back, and two parents have also complained, although three other parents have said what a treat it is to hold a thought-provoking conversation with their child. I have temporarily brought my project to a halt and I am anxious about continuing.

What is my concern?

I am worried that my well-intentioned efforts have come to grief. I am still convinced that children should think critically and question taken-for-granted assumptions, but clearly some other people do not share my opinion.

Why am I concerned?

I am wondering whether my convictions about the need for critical think-ing are rooted in my own bias. I am wondering why some colleagues and parents have complained. What do they know that I don't? What am I not getting?

What kind of evidence do I produce to show why I am concerned?

I can ask the children to write down what they say in other classes. I can keep field notes of what colleagues say to me. I have the notes from the two parents stating that their children are talking back to them. I also have the comments from the three parents who were pleased with their children's intellectual progress.

What can I do about it?

I must check out my own thinking around these things. I can talk with trusted colleagues about what I am doing in teaching the children to think critically. I can ask my two offended colleagues exactly what the children said and why this gives them concern. I can do some reading around critical thinking and critical pedagogies and see what theorists have to say about this. I can think carefully about my own philosophy of education and whether my practices really are rooted in my values. I can talk with the principal about how she understands the educational mission of our school, and whether my actions are fulfilling or contradicting that mission. I can think carefully about the politics of classroom control. Is this enough? Should I stop teaching my children to think critically? I will ask the three supportive parents to comment further – this may give me moral support. I will maintain my reflective diary throughout.

What will I do?

I will do all of the above, but I will not stop teaching the children to think critically. This is the bedrock of my teaching. I hope a possible option is not that I leave teaching.

What kind of evidence do I produce to show that what I am doing is influencing my own learning and the learning of others?

I hope I will gather some data from these different sources to show whether my assessment of the degree of upset is correct, and whether the children are in fact being cheeky or are expressing an honest opinion. I can draw on data from my conversations with trusted colleagues and from my reflective journal about my thoughts around critical thinking, and whether these ideas and values are justifiable. Perhaps I will find that I need to learn more about other people's sensitivities and also about how to manage innovation that may challenge established norms.

How do I evaluate my possible influence?

I hope I will develop increased insight into the values base of critical thinking. I hope I will learn how to manage the situation better. I hope I will learn how to teach children to express their opinions in a thoughtful, non-challenging manner – in other words, to become diplomatic and politically aware. I will aim to gather data that will show, I hope, the development of these insights, and use those data as the basis of the evidence I will produce to justify resuming my abandoned project.

How do I ensure that any judgements I make are reasonably fair and accurate?

I am not certain whether I will be able to ensure this. I can ask my trusted colleagues for their opinion, but I don't think their responses will give me an overall picture. Perhaps I will just have to wait and see whether the complaints continue, or whether the previously complaining members of staff and parents stop complaining. Perhaps the proof of the pudding will come when they congratulate the children for improved learning.

How do I modify my practice in the light of my evaluation?

In writing down my action plan like this I realise that I have embarked on a new action research project, which is about reflecting on my own learning about the situation. I will aim to develop this now into a coherent project. This means that I will have to shelve my first project about teaching children how to think critically and concentrate on understanding the situation first, so that I can perhaps return to the first project at a later date.

CHAPTER 3

Putting your plans into action

Now you need to put your plans into action in relation to social action and in relation to your learning. This chapter helps you to do that. It is in two parts:

1 Putting your plans into action in relation to social action

2 Putting your plans into action in relation to your learning.

Please bear in mind that these two aspects are always interrelated and complementary. Although they are presented here in separate sections for purposes of analysis they should never be seen as free-standing or independent. Learning arises from action and feeds back into the action as an ongoing action–reflection cycle. Reflective practice is made up of social action and learning.

Chapter 2 offered advice about developing action plans that will help you keep the research in perspective and keep you on task. It is easy to get side-tracked. Although the issue you have identified is important, it is tempting to explore other interesting aspects that emerge, so try to stay focused on your main issue and leave the others until later.

1 PUTTING YOUR PLANS INTO ACTION IN RELATION TO SOCIAL ACTION

Your action plan in relation to social action is:

- *What is my concern?* What am I interested in researching? What do I hope to find out?

- *Why am I concerned?* Why is this an important issue for me?

- *What kind of evidence do I produce to show the situation as it is?* What kind of data do I need to gather in order to show clearly what is happening? What kind of evidence do I need to generate?
- *What can I do about the situation?* What are my options?
- *What will I do?* Which option will I choose? What do I intend to do now?
- *What kind of evidence do I produce to show the situation as it unfolds?* What kind of data do I need to gather to show the evolving action? What kind of evidence do I need to generate?
- *How do I show that any conclusions I come to are reasonably fair and accurate?* When I say that something has happened, how do I show that I am justified in claiming this, and not expressing an opinion or making it up?
- *How do I modify my practice in the light of my evaluation?* What do I do differently? How do I understand this point as the end of one course of action and the beginning of a new one?

Here are some ideas about how you can put this plan into action.

What is my concern? What am I interested in researching? What do I hope to find out?

Identify an issue that is occupying your attention at the moment, something that you need to do something about. Beginning something means that you intend to take action, even though you may not be clear what the action will be. The issue you identify could be something to do with yourself – perhaps you need to understand how to manage your time more effectively – or with someone else – perhaps one of the children or another teacher is being bullied.

Keep the issue close to home. It is not helpful at this point to say that your concern is the national policy for how money is being allocated to schools, or how education currently has a narrow technical focus. The wish to do something about these issues may drive your long-term vision for your proposed action (page 8), but you cannot influence them in the next few weeks. At this point stay small, stay focused, and identify an issue that can act as the first steps in addressing that longer-term vision.

Here are some examples of a research issue:

- Managing your time more effectively
- Improving your work as a head of department
- Improving relationships with a colleague.

Aim to articulate your concern as a provisional research question. Remember that social science questions are about what other people are doing ('What are those people doing?'), while action research questions are about what you are doing ('What am I doing?') – recognising that you are always in company with others.

Relate your questions to your research issue, and state your intention to take action in terms of 'How do I . . .?':

Rearch issue	Research question
Managing my timekeeping	How do I manage my time more effectively?
Improving my work as head of department	How do I improve my work as head of department?
Improving relationships with a colleague	How do I relate better to my colleague?

Your questions may use a different form of words, such as:

- What can I do to improve . . .?
- I wonder what would happen if . . .?
- Might it be better if I . . .?

The main points to bear in mind when formulating a research question are:

- This research is about what you are doing, not about what other people are doing.
- You can do something about the situation, and aim to do it.
- You are not searching for final answers or outcomes, just better ways of doing things.
- Your learning in itself is as important an outcome as any changes in classroom or school practice.

Don't worry if you can't articulate your question immediately. Questions tend to emerge as people work their way through their action research. You do need to have a reasonably clear idea of the issue you are addressing though. Also don't worry if your research question changes as the research progresses. This is a common experience. For example, the question 'How do I help my students understand the subject matter?' may change to 'How do I explain the subject matter in a way that all students will understand it?'; and 'How do I get children to be more punctual?' may change to 'How do I ensure that lessons are so interesting that children will want to get to class on time?'

Why am I concerned? Why is this an important issue for me?

Why is this issue important to you? Why is it occupying so much of your thinking time? Perhaps you are in a fulfilling situation and you want to celebrate it. You can already say that you are practising in a way that you feel is right, so you want to describe and explain what is happening. All the children in one of your classes have scored well on their SATs because you deliberately set out to encourage them in special ways, and you feel your strategy has worked. You want to show what you did and why you did it so that others can see how you have evaluated your work and can learn from you. On the other hand, perhaps something is happening that is contrary to what you believe in. The majority of the children in another class are not doing well academically because they are being disrupted by a small group of persistently aggressive children. You have tried to control the group but so far to no avail. You could now say that your educational values are being denied, and you want to do something so that you can work in a way that is more in line with your values and principles.

Sometimes you may find that your research is inspired by this sense that things are not going as you wish. You may find it useful to articulate this in terms of experiencing yourself as a living contradiction when your educational values are not realised in practice (Whitehead 1989). Your research then becomes an exploration of how you can come to live in the direction of your educational values. How do you involve inactive students in lessons and fulfil your values of democratic participation as a key to learning? As a principal, how do you involve all staff in collaborative decision-making? Documenting these processes means gathering data on an ongoing basis to show the situation where your values are denied in practice to a situation where the values are more fully realised.

What kind of evidence do I produce to show the situation as it is? What kind of data do I need to gather in order to show clearly what is happening? What kind of evidence do I need to generate?

Debates about evidence-based practice are strong in current climates of public accountability because, as professionals, teachers need to hold themselves responsible for their work. Most teachers would rightly say that they are doing a good job, but if they claim this they must be prepared to back up the claim with concrete evidence. It is not enough just to say that you are competent. You also need to show that you are justified in saying so.

Some debate exists about what counts as evidence and what standards are used to judge the quality of evidence. The official view is that evidence needs to demonstrate improvement in terms of behavioural outcomes that meet specific targets. Therefore, evidence of successful maths teaching would be the extent to which students achieve improved scores. The outcomes would probably be judged through the analysis of pre- and post-tests results.

Although this kind of statistics-based evidence can be useful, perhaps for diagnostic purposes, it is not particularly helpful for teachers who see learning as more than student performance and teaching as more than imparting specific subject matters. Most teachers enter the profession because they believe they can make a contribution to their students' well-being, mainly by helping them to think for themselves and to create the kind of society they wish to live in. Such educational values are often at odds with the standardised criteria of technical achievement.

To show how you believe you are improving a situation, whether it is the social situation 'out there' or your own learning, you need to monitor what is happening and gather data about significant events. The data will act as a source of evidence (Chapter 5). To monitor the social situation, you would perhaps gather data about what you and your students were doing at the start of your project, and how your students modified their practices in light of their learning with you. You would gather data using field notes, observation schedules, conversations, or any of the other techniques mentioned in Chapter 4. To monitor your learning, you would gather data, perhaps from your research journal, about how you began to think differently, and how this learning influenced what you did in terms of your practice (see Section 2 below).

Evidence is generated from data, so you need to make decisions about what kind of data you are going to gather, where you are going to gather it, and how you are going to analyse and interpret it (Chapter 4 gives detailed advice). At this point you need to have a sense of how you are going to monitor your learning and actions and make judgements about how your learning influences your actions, and how your actions may then influence the way your students learn and act.

What can I do about the situation? What are my options?

You may already have ideas about possible courses of action. If so, you need to identify your best option and pursue it. If you haven't any clear ideas, now may be a good time to ask other people to help.

Bear in mind that this is not a problem-solving exercise, although it involves aspects of problem solving. Margaret Cahill (2000) experienced her practice as a problem because her so-called 'remedial' students were regarded as 'not normal' because their test results for numeracy and literacy fell outside the normative measurement curve. Margaret did not regard her students as problems. To her, they were bright children who had not had the same life chances as other children in mainstream education. For Margaret, the system that categorised them was the problem.

Deciding what to do does not necessarily mean looking for a final answer, because final answers rarely exist. Even when they do exist, answers tend to generate new questions, so any answer needs to be seen as provisional and containing new questions. Try to find new ways forward, and gradually test and see whether your new ways are right for you and the people you are working with. Adopting this research attitude can be difficult because dominant attitudes require people to look for final answers, usually in the form of target-specific outcomes.

While your practice may not present a problem, doing action research is about learning to see your practice as problematic, that is, questioning the way things are, or seem to be. Too often people say, 'This is the way things are because this is the way things are', and many injustices are perpetrated through this attitude: children continue to be labelled as bright or stupid; people continue to be categorised by race, gender and class. Not enough people raise questions about why the situation is as it is and what can be done to transform it so that everyone is seen as a valuable human within a life-affirming context. Bernie Sullivan (2003, 2004) sees the Traveller children for whom she is learning support teacher as a minority ethnic group who are often marginalised by the dominant Settled community. She has demonstrated the value of her inclusional pedagogies to colleagues, and others are trying them out, so school attitudes and practices are changing. Doing action research means learning the value of problematising. Problematising your practice means that you raise questions about why the situation is as it is, and how you can improve it. You consider what you can do, taking a realistic look at your options, and you then decide to act.

What will I do? Which option will I choose? What do I intend to do now?

Having identified a way forward, you now need to try it out. Perhaps you have decided to try a new seating arrangement in class, or pair work in French, or a rotating chair for staff meetings. Whatever you decide to do, use your best creative talents to make it work, but hold the option lightly, because it might not. Exercising this option is not your final decision, but more a matter of testing out an idea to see whether you are exercising your influence in a helpful or harmful way. You need therefore to put in place some monitoring facility to keep track of what you are doing and its effectiveness (see next section).

Bear in mind that you are not working in isolation. You are in direct contact with your students, or immediate colleagues, aiming to influence their learning in an educative way. It is not only about what you do, but also about how you do it. The way that you do something becomes what you do. You can try out a new technique or new arrangement, but techniques and arrangements are about how you are with people and how you all interact. The option you have chosen is a new way of establishing new kinds of relationships. A new seating arrangement means that people will be interacting with one another in new ways; pair work involves people working together more closely than they would by themselves; rotating chairs means that relationships of power shift. Monitoring your work involves observing people's physical actions and reactions and also, more importantly, their relational ones. How are people getting on together? How are they responding to you, and you to them? Are you influencing their learning so that they educate themselves?

Implementing a new strategy also means that you need to take other people in the organisation into consideration. Will your new seating arrangement have implications for other colleagues? Will pair work raise the volume so that next door's reading time is interrupted? Will the rotating chair mean that reticent members of staff will feel forced to take part? Planning to try out a new strategy involves imagining what might be the consequences for all, yourself included, and taking appropriate action.

How do I monitor the situation as it unfolds? What kind of data do I need to gather to show the evolving action? What kind of evidence do I need to generate?

This section contains some general advice about monitoring, gathering data and generating evidence. Chapters 4 and 5 go into more detail.

Monitoring the situation

Monitoring the situation means putting in place some means of observing and keeping records. You can do this yourself, or you can ask other people to help you. If you do it yourself, you need to devise ways of keeping records of what both you and other people are doing and your responses to one another. You can maintain a log or research journal, or you can audio- or videotape the action, or take photos. You can conduct conversations and interviews to gauge reactions to your actions, or ask people to draw pictures or write their responses. You could also ask your critical friends and other colleagues, or your principal, to observe you working with your students and record actions and reactions. Students can act as observers and keep records of what is happening and their responses. It can be valuable to invite parents and caregivers to observe and give their responses.

Aim to do this regularly and over the whole period of the research project. Decide how often you should gather data, whether every day, or every three days, or every week. Use your own sense about this. If your project lasts three weeks, you would need to gather data every two or three days. If it goes on for three months, once a week may be enough. The point is to keep records so that you can make judgements later about whether or not progress has been made in students' learning, and whether your influence has helped that learning.

Your corpus of data is stored in your data archive. This archive could be a box or a drawer, your briefcase or your computer files. Aim to keep your data tidy. Sort it regularly into appropriate categories, such as 'conversations' or 'interviews', and put these into different files or containers. Keeping tidy as you go is more helpful in the long run than putting everything into a box any old how.

Gathering data

Decide which data you are going to gather as early as possible. Decide what you are looking for, and then look for it. Most researchers gather too much data to begin with, and focus down as the research progresses. Don't worry if you seem to be gathering too much. It can be discarded later on if necessary.

Aim to gather data with an eye to your research question. Asking questions about the quality of relationships among your students means thinking about what kinds of change you may see. You could identify two students who you think are representative of the situation you are investigating and monitor their actions, noting any special aspects of their relationships. Or, if you are finding ways of increasing student participation in your classroom through new seating arrangements, you could identify a group of six students and monitor their interactions in various seating arrangements. Your questions about staff engagement could involve monitoring the actions and reactions of three colleagues during staff meetings.

Ask research questions in relation to your values. The question 'How do I encourage good relationships in my class?' is inspired by your commitment to quality relationships in teaching and learning situations. The question 'How do I encourage more participation in my classroom?' is grounded in a commitment to sustainable learning though active participation in conversations. The question 'How do I encourage all staff to take an active role in meetings?' draws on the values of inclusion, justice and relation. These values can come to act as the standards by which you make professional judgements about your work. Can you show that you are living in the direction of your values of quality relationships, participation, inclusion and justice? Making these values explicit will help you focus on which data to gather, and then generate evidence from the data.

Wherever possible, get authentication for your data. Ask people to sign and date your records, and do so yourself. If you transcribe a tape-recorded conversation with your students, ask them to countersign your own signature and date. Any outside observer can then see that you are not fudging your data. Ask parents to sign and date photographs of their children in interaction with you. This kind of authentication lends validity to the data, and is essential for when you come to select pieces of data as evidence.

Generating evidence

Evidence is not the same as data. This point is discussed in Chapter 6, but just to note here that the idea of evidence refers to those special pieces of data that you pull out of your data archive to support or question any claim to knowledge you make. If you say that the quality of relationships has improved between you and your students, which special pieces of data show this claim in action? If you say that participation has increased, which pieces of data can you produce to show how participation has increased over time and in response to certain conditions? If you say that participation in staff meetings has increased, which pieces of data will show who is participating more? These selected pieces of data now stand as evidence.

It is important to bear in mind that the data you look at in your search for evidence may show that the belief you are holding is mistaken. Perhaps you see this for yourself, or perhaps it has been brought to your attention by a critical friend or a validation group. In this case you cannot claim that your data contain evidence that supports your claim to knowledge. Or perhaps you can use the evidence to show that you are aware that your original belief was mistaken, and explain that you have now modified your belief and your claim to knowledge. This would be a powerful way of showing how you have learned in and through action. Episodes where you find that your belief is mistaken can be hard to cope with, but they are a common experience and a great opportunity for new learning.

Once you have generated your evidence, you will present it to your validation group for them to agree (or not) whether they feel your claim is justified (Chapter 5).

How do I show that any conclusions I come to are reasonably fair and accurate? When I say that something has happened, how do I show that I am justified in claiming this, and not simply expressing an opinion?

Doing research is a process of finding out something that was not known before, and claiming that you have done so. If you make a claim that something has happened without producing authenticated evidence, you risk being seen as making it up. Evidence is a core aspect of research. If your evidence does not stand up to scrutiny, people will probably not endorse your claim to knowledge and you may have to go back and think again.

How do I modify my practice in the light of my evaluation? What do I do differently? How do I understand this stage as the end of one course of action and the beginning of a new one?

If you believe that you are achieving your goals, you will probably continue working in this way, but you are not likely to stay like this for long. Good practice means constantly monitoring, evaluating and changing as appropriate. Never be content to leave things as they are. Once you do that, you fall asleep. Good practice means constantly being alert to new possibilities and actively seeking out new opportunities.

Education is about learning and growth and new beginnings. Edward Said (1975) says that each beginning contains intention, which becomes the methodology. Each beginning contains its own methodology within it-self. Each new moment contains the future. We all need to imagine what kind of future we wish to have, and to act now to make the possible prob-able (Joan Whitehead 2003). The future is not something abstract 'out there'. It is already here, in this moment. What we do with this moment is what counts.

If each moment contains its own potential future already within itself, then also each action research cycle contains a potentially unlimited number of new cycles. As your practice unfolds, so you need constantly to maintain your vigilance to ensure that it is as you wish it to be. This atti-tude may get you into difficulties if you work in an organisation driven by bureaucratic values, because those in charge may wish you to implement policy rather than engage in creative practice. Will you give in to bureau-cratic pressure and do as you are told, or will you create a quality learning experience for yourself and the people in your company?

2 PUTTING YOUR PLANS INTO ACTION IN RELATION TO YOUR LEARNING

Developing an action plan in relation to your learning involves asking these kinds of reflective questions:

- What is my concern (about what I know)? What do I need to learn?

- Why am I concerned (about what I know)? Why is this an important issue for me?

- What kind of evidence do I produce to show my concern (about what I know and what I need to learn?)

- What can I do about it (about what I know)? How do I critique what I know? How am I going to learn more?

- What will I do about it?

- What kind of evidence do I produce to show the potential influence of my learning?

- How do I ensure that any judgements I make about my learning and the learning of others are reasonably fair and accurate?

- How do I modify my practice in the light of my new learning? How do my practice and my learning develop together?

Here are some ideas about how you can put this plan into action.

What is my concern (about what and how I know)? What do I need to learn?

Being prepared to be open to new learning, and to monitor and evaluate it, means you appreciate that learning underpins and informs practice. You are prepared to problematise your work, that is, not accept that 'This is the way things are because this is the way things are.' You intend to check out whether you should accept that this should be the way things are. This means not only thinking about what you do and how you do it, but also thinking about what you know and how you have come to know. You are problematising your thinking as well as your actions, which is a difficult thing to do, and also courageous. Problematising one's thinking is risky because once you begin thinking differently you can never go back to your old ways, but it is essential if you claim to be a reflective practitioner. Expressing your concern about how you think and learn means stating your intent to learn new ways and evaluate them. You do this in relation to your values.

For example, Rosalie Doherty, a Women's Health Officer, encouraged providers to reflect on how they thought about gender issues in the work-place (Doherty 2004). Jacinta Davenport, a participating teacher in the adult education service, wrote in her research report:

> Through my reading and discussions . . . I reflected on my interpretation of gender for the first time. Prior to this I never considered how gender is socially constructed and maintained for men and women alike. I saw gender as fixed and immovable. I accepted the gender stereotypes as they were . . . For the first time I am asking questions:
> - Do I as a woman do what is best for me or what is 'expected of me' in society?
> - Do I reinforce female stereotypes in my behaviour, attitudes, values and expectations?
>
> As I write this, I realise that if I am honest I am afraid of raising these issues publicly in case I will be associated with being a 'feminist'. I realise now with embarrassment that I have associated gender with 'women fighting for their rights' and that this had had a negative resonance in me. My thinking and behaviour up to now has reflected the social norm that I never stopped to reflect upon or challenge. I have written in my reflective diary:
>
> 'I now realise that I have continued to reinforce accepted gender roles in my personal and professional life through fear and ignorance. From now on I am going to be more active in raising awareness through modelling and promoting gender fair behaviour, being fair to both men and women.'
>
> (Davenport 2004)

Moira Cluskey (1996) also tells in her story how her growing awareness of gender issues informed her practice. You can read her story on http://www.jeanmcniff.com and in her dissertation (Cluskey 1997).

Why am I concerned (about what I know)? Why is this an important issue for me?

All too often people, including teachers, are expected to do as they are told and not to question orders. Teachers should accept what is presented as official knowledge and policy (Apple 1993) and apply it to their practice. However, many teachers wish to live their lives in education in terms of truth, justice and beauty. They wish to enable young people to think creatively and to exercise their capacity for questioning and critique. Teachers therefore also have to exercise their own capacity for questioning and critique. Rather than accept official knowledge and policy, many teachers aim to engage critically with it and question its underpinning assumptions. Consequently, when you raise questions about what you are doing in relation to your practice, especially about whether you are living in the direction of your values or someone else's, you also raise questions around whether you are engaging critically with underpinning assumptions, both your own and other people's. Are you practising in a way that is commensurate with your values? Are you thinking in a way that enables you to critique and problematise your practice? If you are, how do you show it? If you are not, how do you learn to change it?

What kind of evidence do I produce to show my concern (about what I know and what I need to learn)?

You can document how you think and the changes in your ways of thinking most obviously by means of your journal and accounts of practice.

Right from the beginning of your project, aim to keep a research journal. Note key episodes during the research in relation to what you are doing, such as when you formulate your research question, or gather some important data. Particularly note what this means in terms of your learning. Why is formulating your research question important? Why is that particular piece of data so significant?

You can keep track of your actions and learning by organising your journal to address these questions:

- What have I done?
- What have I learned?

- What is the significance of the learning?
- How do I develop my practice in the light of my learning?

You can organise your journal as you wish. You could draw four columns across one or two pages (see Figure 4.1 on page 73), or you could write regular entries, addressing the questions in turn (see the example below). Make your own decisions about whether to comment on the significance of your learning in relation to individual actions, or to look at your actions as mini-sequences over a period of time and then comment on them as blocks of action.

You may also reflect on what you have written up to now about your practice. Use existing reports about what you currently do and think (such as memos) as data, and draw on these to show the development of your learning through your enquiry.

For example, suppose you are looking at how you teach. You are concerned that you seem to do most of the talking in class. You wrote a memo to a colleague last week saying, 'I worry that I do most of the talking in class, but I have to cover the syllabus. How do I get the children to take a more active role? How do I get them to ask the right kinds of question?' You decide to make this an issue and actively begin exploring ways of getting the children to ask the kinds of question that will also ensure that they acquire the appropriate subject knowledge. After one such episode you record the following.

- *What have I done?* I have listened carefully to each child, asking them what they understood about what they read.

- *What have I learned?* I have learned that I have to listen more and ask prompting questions that will help give the children capacity and confidence to ask questions themselves.

- *What is the significance of my learning?* I have learned how important it is to get the children to ask questions themselves and to engage with their own learning.

- *How do I develop my practice in the light of my learning?* I will ask more questions from now on. I will aim to give fewer answers myself. I have learned the importance of allowing the children to learn by asking questions. I have come to understand my practice as asking questions, rather than giving answers.

These kinds of comment can act as powerful evidence when you come to claim that you have improved your practice by developing student-centred pedagogies.

What can I do about it (about what I know)? How do I critique what I know? How am I going to learn more?

Problematising one's practice and developing new ways of knowing is hard, because it means thinking about how you think, and being prepared to change it. It means becoming critical, not only about what other people do and say, but also about what you do and say and, especially, interrogating the assumptions that underpin what you do and say.

For example, as a principal you decide to undertake an action enquiry into how you can raise the level of student and staff attendance in school, because maximum attendance would be seen as an indicator of a successful school, and you want to be seen as successful. How do you do this?

Perhaps the first thing to do is question your own assumptions about why attendance is low. Are people staying away because they are lazy or recalcitrant or want to do a part-time job? Or are they staying away because school is not such an attractive place to be? Whose responsibility is it to encourage them to come to school? Perhaps, instead of asking, 'How do I ensure maximum attendance?', you need to ask, 'How do I ensure that school is the kind of place that people will want to be in?'

Asking self-reflective and self-critical questions is at the heart of action research, because asking these kinds of questions shows how we are holding ourselves accountable for what we do. Monitoring and recording how you move from asking unproblematic kinds of questions to more critical questions can show your own process of learning.

What kind of evidence do I produce to show the potential influence of my learning?

Keeping your reflective journal is one valuable way of showing the development of your learning. Another powerful way is to produce your accounts of practice, and to interweave commentaries about your action with commentaries about your learning in and from action.

Your accounts of practice can be in written or multimedia form, and you can be creative in how you express these different aspects. For example, in written documents you may choose to use one font to tell the story of your action and another font, perhaps also in a different colour, to give a reflective commentary on what you have learned from the action (see the example on page 74). In multimedia presentations you may choose to insert a video clip into your text to show the living reality of the point you are making, or you may introduce still photographs, or link to another website, to develop a point (see Glenn 2003).

How do I ensure that any judgements I make about my learning and the learning of others are reasonably fair and accurate?

Producing your account of learning becomes more than a simple account of action. You explain how you are learning in the practice about the practice, and how you are reconceptualising and reconfiguring your own learning about practice. You are producing and making explicit your ideas as a theory of practice. You can claim that you are developing your own original theory of practice, and you can produce evidence from your documentary accounts to show your process of theorising and its evolutionary nature. This is an exciting thing to do, and it communicates that teachers can and should produce their theories of practice, and make these available to public scrutiny in the interests of professional accountability.

This has major implications for the idea of evidence-based practice. By undertaking your action enquiry you are aiming to show how you have improved your practice and that it is not mere activity. Your work is morally engaged and committed praxis. You are able to show how you have transformed practice into praxis by explaining how you have learned to critique the thinking that informed your practice, and you can produce evidence to show that this is the case.

How do I modify my practice in the light of my new learning? How do my practice and my learning develop together?

How do you show that your critical thinking has led to new improved practices? How do you explain the way in which your new practices are improvements on old ones? You need to explain the significance of your work to others. If you don't show that you understand why your work is important, why should they take you seriously?

The significance of your research is in relation to how you have learned to live your values more fully in your practice, and that you know how you have done so. You are making your knowledge public so that other people can learn with and from you. You are not saying that you have got it right for all time. You are saying that you have got it right for now, and tomorrow is another day. You will change, along with the changing world you live in. Your new practice will raise new questions and new challenges, and you will learn how to deal with them. Doing action research enables people to develop ways of thinking about life as always in process and always raising new questions, and they learn to challenge dominant attitudes that say we must work towards closure and tidy answers. If you can do this you will really show the power of action research – a form of enquiry that resists closure and celebrates life in all its uncertainty and insistence on new beginnings. You are unique, and so is your practice. You have never existed before and you never will again. This is your opportunity to shine and encourage others to shine with you. Go for it, and enjoy the limelight.

SUMMARY

This chapter has outlined possible ways of putting your plans into action in relation to action and in relation to learning. We do emphasise that these two aspects are always complementary and symbiotic.

In the next chapter we look at issues of gathering and interpreting data. This is a vital step in producing evidence, which you will need to show both the current situation as it is and also the situation as it unfolds, so that you can show how your learning 'in here' is having some influence on the social situation 'out there'. What you are learning has deep implications for how others may learn and come to new understandings of how they also can improve their practices.

CHAPTER 4

Monitoring, gathering and interpreting data

This chapter deals with monitoring your practice and learning, so that you can gather and interpret the kind of data that can later be turned into evidence. The chapter is in two parts:

1 Monitoring practice, and gathering and interpreting data about your action

2 Monitoring practice, and gathering and interpreting data about your learning.

Each section gives advice about who does the action, what is done, and how it is done.

Remember that research is undertaken to produce new knowledge. The best action research projects are those that lead to a situation where researchers can say that they have generated new knowledge about both practice and learning. In their reports they explain how they are contributing to new practices and new understandings, and they produce evidence from within the data to support their claims. The implications for you are that you need to keep an eye on what kind of data you are gathering and how it will be interpreted so that you can later extract evidence from it. [To note: You can say 'data is' or 'data are'. Both are acceptable. In this book we tend to say 'data is', with occasional uses of 'data are' as seems appropriate.]

1 MONITORING PRACTICE AND GATHERING DATA ABOUT YOUR ACTION

This section offers advice, first about monitoring, and second about gathering and interpreting data.

1 Monitoring your action

Monitoring is about keeping track of what is happening. Remember that the focus of the action is you, so the aim is to monitor what you are doing. Remember also that you are in relation with others and trying to influence their learning, so monitoring what they are doing and learning is important, because you are going to show how you are improving your work in relation to how they are improving theirs.

Questions arise around:

- Who monitors?
- What is monitored?
- How is it monitored?

Here is a summary of the ideas in this section.

Questions	Options
Who monitors?	You alone You and students/other participants External observers
What is monitored?	The potential influence of your actions in relation to others' learning
How is it monitored?	Written methods and recordings Audio-visual methods and recordings

Who monitors?

Decide in advance how far you wish to make this a collaborative project, and the extent to which you may later wish to triangulate your data, that is, compare and contrast your data and your perceptions of the data with the perceptions of others. You can adopt any of the following strategies, and you can also mix and match them.

You alone

You observe and monitor what you are doing. You also observe and monitor what your students or other participants are doing. Remember that it is virtually impossible to keep track of everything at the same time, so you need to be selective. Choose perhaps only two or three participants who you feel will be representative of what you trying to show, such as the extent to which you feel you are exercising your educative influence, and focus on them. When teaching a new concept in geography, say, identify two or three children of different ability, and monitor what they do and say as they engage with learning the concept.

You and students/other participants

You and your students or other participants observe and monitor your own and one another's individual activity. You keep records of what you and they are doing, and your students and other participants keep records of what they and you are doing. At some point you will agree to pool your records and compare and contrast your observations. How do you all monitor the actions in a PE class when students are learning a new skill? How does everyone monitor the interactions in a departmental meeting? Be selective. Decide how many sources are sufficient, and what kind. Too many data can swamp rather than support.

External observers

You invite external observers to observe and monitor what you and/or your students are doing, and submit their reports for your and/or your students' analysis. How do you ensure that they will attend to what you are trying to communicate? Which observers do you trust to observe and monitor you fairly and competently? In problematic cases where, for example, you suspect a parent of abusing their child, or have to inform a parent that you are excluding their child from school, how do you manage the interview with the parent?

What is monitored?

The central focus of your enquiry is your learning and how it influences your activity. Only you can be aware of the internal processes of your own learning, but you and others can observe and monitor the activity that your learning informs, and how it potentially influences your students' learning.

What you observe and monitor needs to be related to your research question. You therefore need to decide two issues in relation to your research question:

- What aspects of your practice will be observed and monitored?
- What aspects of your students' and others' responses will be observed and monitored?

Here are some examples of how this may work.

	What aspects of your practice will be observed and monitored?	What aspects of your students' and others' responses will be observed and monitored?
Example 1 **You are investigating how you can encourage learning.**	What kinds of question do you ask?	How do students respond to your questions? Do they show that they understand what you are asking?
	How do you ensure that students' answers are valued, even if they are inaccurate?	Do students respond in a way that shows they feel good about themselves?
	What kind of language do you use to communicate your feelings?	Do students show that they feel valued from what you say, or are they dejected?
Example 2 **You are investigating how you manage a learning situation.**	Where do you position yourself in your classroom in order to encourage maximum participation from all?	Can all students see you? Do they all feel they are getting a fair chance to answer?
	How do you manage and set up interactions successfully?	Are all students involved? Do they show that they are interested in what each other has to say?
	How do you arrange for variety in pace and activity?	Is the lesson lively? Is everyone alert and engaged?
Example 3 **You are investigating how you can manage meetings more successfully.**	How do you ensure that all voices are encouraged and valued?	Does everyone take part willingly? Do they show that they are pleased when they offer an opinion?
	Do you always act as chair of the meeting?	How do others respond to an invitation to act as chair? Do they manage chairing successfully?
	How do you ensure that accurate records are kept?	Is a minuting secretary appointed? How are minutes kept? Are people assured that they will see the minutes?

How is it monitored?

You have choices around the way you monitor practice and gather data. These include written methods and live methods.

Written methods
These include:

Field notes   These are the jottings you make as you note actions. It is a good idea to keep a small notebook with you, but you can also make field notes on odd bits of paper, or even on the back of your hand. Aim to write them up later in a systematic fashion.

Personal logs and diaries   A diary is used to keep a record both of the action and also of your learning (pages 71–4). Many researchers make too many observations to begin with, but soon narrow the focus as the research develops and the research question firms up. Aim to gather data in relation to your research question.

Questionnaires   Be careful of questionnaires. They are notoriously difficult to construct and should be used with caution. If you do use a questionnaire, do so to get a sense of trends and perspectives, and always view the data you gather from questionnaires with a degree of scepticism. Different forms of questionnaire ask different kinds of questions, such as closed or open questions. You are more likely to get people's opinions through open questions, but responses to open questions are more difficult to analyse than responses to closed questions. It helps to decide in advance what kind of responses you are looking for.

Surveys   The same advice applies. It is not always possible for people to give definitive answers, and responses such as 'Yes, but . . .' are not easily catered for. Surveys can be useful, again to test general trends, but need to be regarded with some caution.

Record sheets   These are records of action that enable you to see at a glance what happened and to analyse the action. You may draw up tables and charts, for example, to indicate who speaks and how often, or how people interact, or how many times you ask a particular question or offer answers.

Live methods
These include:

Interviews   This is where you interview other people to get their perspective on what is happening. You can use paper and pen, audio- or videotape.

The aim is to let people speak for themselves in response to prompts from you. In the same way as with questionnaires and surveys, it is important to ask the right kind of question to get the kind of responses you wish to have. If you want factual information, you can ask closed questions, the kind that elicit 'yes/no' responses. If you are after people's personal opinions, you will ask more open questions that encourage them to speak in broader terms.

Role play   This has developed into a new genre, which is also known as performance text. It is a powerful way of communicating how people respond to one another. If you really want to know how students are responding to your teaching, set up a role play situation where someone substitutes for you and communicates the way they perceive you. Be prepared for some surprises, and also be ready to make some modifications to your practice in light of what you see.

Audio- and videotape recordings   This is as near to live action as it is currently possible to get. Audio tape recordings are valuable for capturing the spontaneity of people expressing their opinions. Videotape recordings capture the action to the extent that you are able to show the quality of what you do and how people respond to you. Sometimes videotape recording is invaluable, especially when your claims are in relation to improving the quality of relationships. You can show the nature of the relationships through the live footage, which is a powerful form of expression and can lend greater weight to establishing the validity of claims to knowledge than words alone.

2 Gathering and interpreting data about your action

You not only have to make decisions about how you will monitor the action in order to gather data; you also have to decide which data you will gather, and how it will later be analysed and interpreted. This issue can be tricky, because interpretation involves ideas about validity, so it becomes a political question about who has the right to interpret the data and make judgements about your work, and whether you agree with their views.

The same questions arise as before:

● Who gathers and interprets data?

● Which data is gathered and interpreted?

● How is the data gathered and interpreted?

Here is a summary of the ideas in this section.

Questions	Options
Who gathers and interprets data?	You alone You and students/other participants External observers
Which data is gathered and interpreted?	Instances of practice that show the influence of your actions in relation to others' learning
How is the data gathered and interpreted?	Written methods and recordings Audio-visual methods and recordings

Who gathers and interprets data?

Decide in advance how far you wish to make this a collaborative project, and the extent to which you wish to triangulate your data, that is, compare and contrast your data and your perceptions of the data with the perceptions of others. You can adopt any of the following strategies, and also mix and match them.

You alone

Aim to gather data about what you are doing and about what your students and other participants are doing. This means watching out for any instances that you believe show your research issue in action and which you wish to capture. If you are working individually to encourage students' motivation, what will you look out for that shows they are more motivated? If you are a member of a team with responsibility for developing a Personal, Social and Health Education programme in school, what kinds of data will you gather that shows growth in personal and social relationships? How will you negotiate your own interpretations of your data with others?

You and students/other participants

Would it be helpful to invite other people to gather data about what you and your students are doing? Getting someone else's opinion on what you are doing can be useful, especially in collaborative projects. If you are working with colleagues to draw up a school policy on Citizenship Education, what will you look out for that shows whether all staff agree on how you understand citizenship or arrange for its inclusion in the curriculum? How will you negotiate your observations with one another?

External observers

If you decide to invite external observers to gather data about your practice, you need to alert them to watch out for what you wish them to see, such as whether, as a head of year, you conduct your conversations with colleagues in a respectful manner, or whether, as a learning support teacher, you ensure that children understand what you are aiming to communicate. Be prepared for some new insights. Often others, seeing through their own eyes, see things that we do not see ourselves, so suddenly facing up to a reality in which you may not be acting in the way you thought you were can be difficult, and will involve your negotiating other people's observations and interpretations with your own. This calls for considerable commitment and courage, but it can be a valuable learning experience.

Which data is gathered and interpreted?

Deciding which data to gather and analyse can be difficult. It can be helpful to keep an eye out for all those instances that are relevant to the issue you are investigating in action.

Here is an example, presented as two episodes that show how the action develops over time.

	Instances of practice where data can be found	Examples of data you can extract, and their sources
Episode 1	You are teaching poetry to a full class. You also have a responsibility to teach personal and social education throughout the curriculum. You want to check whether you are actually teaching personal and social education through poetry, and you experiment with pedagogies, in this case a student mentoring scheme. One of the class, P, a particularly shy girl, seldom says a word, so you partner her with a more confident student, S. You ask them to discuss the poetry and compare their opinions. You keep field notes about when P speaks and what she says.	In your research journal [source of data] you write about how you intend to develop appropriate pedagogies. You read a book about mentoring, and you send a memo [source of data] to your head of department saying that you wish to try out a student mentoring scheme. You note the instances in your field notes [source of data] when P speaks and what she says.

	Instances of practice where data can be found	Examples of data you can extract, and their sources
Episode 2	Over time, you observe that she speaks more often and more freely, and you note these occasions. At the end of a month, you hold a tape-recorded conversation with students R, A, P and her partner S, about how they feel they are making progress in understanding the poetry they are studying, and whether or not they demonstrate increased personal awareness and are confident in relationships.	You make regular diary entries [sources of data] and field notes [sources of data] about when she speaks and what she says.

You hold a tape-recorded conversation [source of data]. |

Here is an excerpt from the conversation:

You How do you feel you are getting on?
S We talk about the poetry.
You What do you think you are learning?
S We are learning about metaphors and similes and how they are used.
R Last week we talked about the similes we could find in Coleridge's poetry.
You Are there many? What do you think, P?
P We found quite a lot.

P speaks with gentle prompting. The whole episode shows students' capacity to engage in a conversation.

Later in the conversation:

You What do you think about this metaphor – 'the trees waved their long hair'?
S It's a lovely metaphor.
P How about 'the dancing trees swayed in the wind'?

P offers her opinion. She shows her knowledge of the idea of metaphor, and also demonstrates her self-confidence in putting her own ideas forward in public.

When you come to write up your research report, you can include excerpts like these in the main body of your text, and you would put the complete transcript of the conversations, as well as the tape itself, in your appendices or your data archive, together with other sources of data such as your research diary and your field notes.

On another occasion you may videotape the group in action without you. As you observe the tape later with the group, you note that P is laughing a lot with two other girls. Her laughter is particularly noticeable because in previous times she barely even smiled. When you write your report you will draw your reader's attention to this episode and comment on its significance. You will place the video or CD-ROM in your appendices or archive.

You can gather data using any or all of the monitoring techniques mentioned above. You will aim to gather data over a designated time during your research, and you will do so at regular intervals. Make sure you date the data as you gather it. You should decide your own schedule. As noted on page 51, perhaps in a project lasting three weeks you would gather data every few days, whereas in a three-month project, every week would be sufficient. Whenever you gather your data you would look out for those particular pieces that show how you are moving towards addressing your research question and, by implication, how you are living more fully in the direction of your values.

2 MONITORING LEARNING AND GATHERING AND INTERPRETING DATA ABOUT YOUR LEARNING

Just as you monitor and track developments in your actions in the world, you need to do the same for your learning, in relation to your practice. The questions raised above about who monitors, what is monitored and how it is monitored are not so relevant here because it is only you who can directly monitor and comment on your learning, although other people may comment on how your learning seems to have developed in relation to what you say and do.

Self-reflection involves both thinking about what you are doing and also becoming critical about what you are doing. Becoming self-critical means questioning your thinking and how you have come to think like this. For example, you may have used the generic term 'mankind' instead of 'humans' or 'people' without being aware that this usage promotes a form of discourse that privileges males over females. The famous phrase 'One giant step for mankind' does not say much about women's achievements. Use of the politically correct term 'people of colour' itself automatically differentiates people with dark skins from people with light skins, suggesting that white is the norm, and so potentially contributes to discourses of alienation rather than to discourses that celebrate a common humanity. Thinking in a self-critical way can be a new form of thinking in itself, and can generate new perceptions of previously taken-for-granted situations. This new thinking it-self has to be tested and modified, so that it can feed back into new practices. How do you check whether your use of 'people' or 'humanity' is appropriate in your teaching contexts? How do you engage with people of different ethnic origins? You can often come to do things differently in the world because you are doing things differently in your head. Showing how your learning feeds back into practice, which in turn changes and generates new learning on an ongoing, cyclical basis, is what qualifies you to call yours a self-reflective practice. It is also what enables you to claim that you are making your contribution both to new practices and new knowledge.

For example, Máirín Glenn (2004) writes:

> The original focus of my action research was to investigate the usefulness of internet-based multimedia projects in my primary classroom. One day a colleague asked, 'Why do you work with multimedia? Why is it so important to you?' I couldn't answer. I could describe what I was doing but I couldn't say why I was doing it. I couldn't explain why multimedia were important for learning.
>
> I began to reflect on how my children learn, and also how I, their teacher, learn. I began to see that learning was not only imparting (by me) specific knowledge (to them), but was also in the sharing and creating of our knowledge as we worked together. Multimedia were especially important because they allowed for multiple ways of representing knowledge, for transforming the knowledge into new forms, and for sharing it so that new knowledge could be created.
>
> These insights have led me to develop new relational forms of pedagogics, which recognise my children as powerful knowledge creators and my classroom as the context for a community of practice that can link with other communities by means of the internet.

(see also Glenn 2003)

1 Monitoring your learning

The best way, but not the only way, to monitor your learning is to keep a learning journal. This can be the same journal as your research journal, or a different one. You might choose to keep a research journal in which you note critical incidents in the action, gather data, and comment on progress; and you might also keep a learning journal where you do the same in relation to your learning. Decide what suits you best. Make sure you can identify them easily, and keep them near at hand. Aim to keep them up to date.

Your journal may be of a traditional paper kind, or it could be an audio- or a videotaped journal. These work in the same way as a written journal, except that they are 'live'. You could also keep a multimedia journal, where you insert pictures and video clips to support your written text, which can then act as a powerful source of evidence.

Monitoring your learning means asking these kinds of questions on a systematic basis:

- What have I done?
- What have I learned?
- What is the significance of the learning?
- How will the learning generate new actions?

Here are some further ideas on how this technique may be used.

What have I done?

What have you done in recent practice that is special in terms of the issue you are investigating? You could identify single instances of practice. Perhaps you acted in a new way that encouraged a shy child to interact with others for the first time, as with P (page 68). Perhaps you maintained silence in response to a question when normally you would give an answer. Or you could identify longer episodes of accumulative practice. Perhaps you tried implementing new forms of management structures that were designed to encourage more participative working. Perhaps you worked with others to develop a gender policy in school.

What have I learned?

Think about what you have done and what you have learned from the experience. Perhaps you have learned that encouragement works wonders, or that silence can be as powerful a response as speech. Perhaps you have learned that participative working can be encouraged through the development of appropriate structures, or that implementing a gender policy means first raising awareness and securing the engagement of all staff. Write down, or otherwise record, these learnings.

What is the significance of this learning?

Why is this learning important, and what are its potential implications? Perhaps it is significant in the sense that:

- you have developed greater insights into the issues you are investigating, and understand more clearly the reasons for why you are doing what you are doing at an individual level
- you have developed greater insights into how your work is potentially influencing workplace practices
- you have developed insights into how your learning is encouraging the learning of others and influencing their practice in new ways.

How will my new learning generate new actions?

Think about the relationship between your learning and any new actions. How will you do things differently? What do you need to be aware of? Most importantly, how do you show the seamlessly integrated nature of your learning and actions, so that you really can claim that yours is a form of self-reflective practice?

Some people keep a record of this kind of reflection on action as a written text, in the same way as it is presented here. Others choose to write it up across one or two pages (see Figure 4.1), which they have divided into columns, headed 'What have I done?' (or 'What happened?', or 'Action'), 'What have I learned?' (or 'Learning' or 'Reflection'), 'What is the significance of this learning?' (or 'Significance'), and 'How will my learning generate new actions?' (or 'New action' or 'Implications'). Computer software can help you devise exciting layouts using a variety of templates, fonts and colours, or clip-art 'think bubbles'. You decide what is right for you. Be imaginative and adventurous. There is no right or wrong way, except what is right for you.

What have I done? or What happened? or Action	What have I learned? or Learning or Reflection	What is the significance of this learning? or Significance	How will my learning generate new actions? or New action or Implications

Figure 4.1   Example of a page divided into four sections

You can also monitor your own learning through your progress and final reports. Throughout your accounts it is important to comment both on your action and the learning involved, and to show how learning arose from within the action and fed back into the action. You could use one font for communicating the action and another font for communicating your reflection, as in this example from a progress report from Mary Roche (Roche 2004), as she recounts how she encourages five-year-old children to think critically.

The children and I gathered into our circle for Thinking Time and I began by reading a poem about rainbow colours. The children as usual started to respond by asking their questions about why things were as they were, and how they might be different.

Danny   I wonder where a rainbow's colours come from?

Amy   A rainbow's got only happy colours.

Colm   I know the answer to Danny's question. It's an upside-down smile. You can see it the right way up in Australia because my auntie lives there. The sky is smiling because the rain is gone. Clouds hate being grey because it's boring.

Brid   I disagree. Clouds and the sky don't feel. I think it's just because the rain has washed the sky and the sun lets us see lots of bright colours.

Mary's reflection

I wonder where these ideas came from? Did I communicate them to the children? Did they read them from fairy stories? Colm is, as usual, quite dogmatic; Brid seems to have the beginnings of scientific thinking in her notion that sunlight and rain are both somehow involved in making rainbows.

Encourage your students and other participants to develop the same strategies. This can be a powerful way to encourage their learning, and people, you included, can share their learning journals and accounts (with permission), and learn from one another. Sharing accounts with other colleagues can also be a powerful form of staff development and school improvement.

Gathering data about your learning

The data that show your learning can also be drawn from the data you gather about your practice. So, for example, you could take the instance where P began interacting with others as a key piece of data, and reflect on that.

Data about your learning and its potential significance can be found in a variety of places, including the following:

Observations from practice   You observe and monitor practice, and note key incidents.

Observations from reviewing records of practice   Perhaps when you look at a videotape for the second time you note episodes that you did not notice before.

Conversations with others   These can be tape recorded or otherwise. Remember that you can reconstruct these conversations if you did not keep a record of them at the time.

Field notes   These are the notes you make while in the 'field', such as during a lesson or meeting.

Letters and other exchanges   Perhaps a colleague perceives from what you say that you seem to be thinking differently.

Your diary   As you read an entry perhaps it takes on a new significance in light of later actions and reflections.

Synthesising

Be aware that this chapter breaks down different aspects and analyses them, so it may appear that aspects may be understood as separate from one another. This kind of analysis is important and can be helpful, but it is not the whole story. No one aspect is separate from another. When you produce your report you will also find that to a certain extent you present things in an analytical way, but it is important to emphasise that the practice you are reporting is holistic and integrated.

Your action can be seen as the manifestation of your learning, and can also generate new learning. The learning feeds back into new action. The world 'in here' and the world 'out there' are complementary and symbiotic.

This point is crucial in new debates in educational research about the relationships of practice and theory. Traditionally, practice and theory were seen as separate. Newer thinking sees practice as a form of theory (Dadds and Hart 2001; Schön 1995; Whitehead 1989, 2000). By producing your account of practice, and explaining how your claims are rigorously validated, you are showing how teachers' professional learning can be seen as a powerful form of theorising that is guided by the highest educational principles.

SUMMARY

Chapters 2, 3 and 4 have set out the practicalities of doing action research. Three case studies now follow that show how the advice can be turned into practice.

The first two case studies are written by Ma Hong and Gong Lixia, who are teacher-educators in China's new Experimental Centre for Educational Action Research in Foreign Languages Teaching, in Guyuan Teachers' College, Guyuan, 756000, Ningxia Province. These case studies demonstrate that educators the world over can benefit from drawing up action plans and pursuing an action enquiry in a systematic way. The studies are also important because they are written within a context where China has introduced a New Curriculum that emphasises the development of student-centred pedagogies in foreign languages teaching. This means a departure from traditional didactic pedagogies, and also has deep implications for the kind of relationships that teachers will aim to develop with their students. These issues are evident within the case studies. You can also read more about the work from Moira Laidlaw's story on pages 120–123, and also from Moira's writings (see, for example, Laidlaw 2004; Tian and Laidlaw 2004). Full versions of the case studies are available at http://www.actionresearch.net/moira.shtml

The third case study is by Lisa Percy, who undertook her action enquiry as part of her Master's degree programme at the University of Bath.

CASE STORY 1: HOW CAN I HELP MY STUDENTS TO IMPROVE THEIR ENGLISH?

Ma Hong

I am a teacher of English in China, and have been teaching for two years. I undertook my professional learning within a traditional context, which emphasised that teachers should help their students learn correct answers and achieve a high standard of language proficiency. This involved using pedagogies that put the responsibility for success on the teacher's teaching, rather than on the students' learning. Using this approach also meant that my students and I were exhausted at the end of each day. I wondered what I could do about the situation. In 2003 I heard from my colleague Tao Rui about the action research approaches she was developing under the guidance of Moira Laidlaw at the Guyuan Teachers' College, so I asked Moira to help me develop new pedagogies. Under Moira's guidance I began my formal action enquiry within the context of my class of 40 English-major students aged 15–18, of which 98% had failed the entrance examination for senior middle school. I met them for a two-hour class three times a week.

This report sets out the action–reflection steps I took to develop my enquiry.

What was my concern?

The level of proficiency of 80% of the students in spoken and written English was unsatisfactory. They had limited vocabulary, could not pronounce even simple words, understood little when I used English as my teaching medium, and could not use the basic grammar they had learned in junior middle school. I wanted to help them develop confidence, show more initiative and become more motivated to learn English. I decided to monitor the progress of the whole class, focusing especially on three students, Ma Jie, Ma Fei and Yu Jinghu, whose level of proficiency was representative of the low achievers. I felt that if I could help them, I could help others also.

Why was I concerned?

Three reasons drove my enquiry. The first was my desire to help the whole class to concentrate more on their learning, rather than spend time chatting and wasting time. The second reason was to improve my own teaching methods. The students were still in a traditional mode of learning passively, waiting to be told what to do, and were unwilling to answer questions in public for fear of losing face if they made a mistake. I seemed to be doing the work for them, rather than enabling them to practise and think for themselves. Third, I could empathise with the experience of being a less able student because I had also had that experience at school and had achieved my current position through sheer hard work and determination. I knew how important it was for all students to feel cared for by their teacher.

What could I do?

I wanted to:

- create a friendly, well-disciplined, united class spirit
- help students develop confidence in themselves
- encourage them to take more responsibility for their learning.

Who could help me?

I could observe lessons given by Moira, and colleagues Li Peidong, Tao Rui and others. I could ask them to observe my lessons and offer critical feedback.

What did I do?

I developed several strategies.

1   To overcome students' anxieties about speaking in front of the class, I divided the whole class into eight groups. Each group nominated a leader who was proficient and confident in English. They could practise among themselves, calling on my help when necessary. I found that many students became more confident and proactive. One of my special participants, Ma Jie, one day volunteered to answer a question for the first time.

2   I developed strategies to encourage students to take the initiative about their learning, and to ask questions as well as offer answers.

3   I paid particular attention to encouraging effort. I praised them publicly, and wrote encouraging comments in their books. When a less able student answered correctly I got the whole class to applaud them. I also encouraged them to regard mistakes as opportunities for learning. It took a long time to persuade them that I was genuine about this, because our culture regards making mistakes as a loss of face. This was one of the most difficult aspects of my new pedagogies, but students responded well.

4   I encouraged students also by taking an interest in their family stories. Many less able students come from rural environments, where opportunities for schooling are rare. We talked about how hard their parents and families worked to enable them to come to college, and about how important it was for them to succeed. I showed that I cared about the honour of the class, and I showed that I was prepared to work as hard

as they were. We developed good relationships, and soon the spirit of the class became one of collaborative working through a respectful atmosphere.

5   I aimed to make my teaching more interesting. Rather than teaching rules of grammar, I made up short stories that contained examples of the rules in action. Students were asked to listen to the stories, and work out the rules for themselves. I set them short exercises, and organised them into groups to share their learning. Because these were new methodologies for me, I asked them for feedback, and they said that they found this way of learning interesting and enjoyable.

6   I shifted the emphasis from learning rules to practising language. I varied the exercises according to students' ability.

7   I expressed my pleasure and gratitude to my students. I thanked the group leaders for helping others. They in turn took their duties seriously, and checked with their peers whether they had understood the task and volunteered extra help where appropriate. I valued this aspect particularly, because it met my own values of the need for moral teaching and the value of hard work and care for others.

How can I evaluate my work?

I used the following strategies to get feedback on the effectiveness of my work.

- I kept field notes about when students volunteered to speak. I noted much increased activity and confidence among all the students.

- I invited group leaders to keep journals, and asked their permission to access their journals for evidence about my influence. The journals contain comments such as:
  'I made progress in dictation this time.'
  'Our group members became more and more active in asking questions.'
  'Everyone in our group works hard, and sometimes there were even too many questions for me, so they went to ask other leaders . . .'

- I held conversations with students. They said that the atmosphere in class encouraged them to learn.

- I distributed a questionnaire. Thirty-five students felt that they had made significant progress. Their comments included:
  'I feel I am much better.'
  'I am making progress though I am still not good at English.'
  'Thanks for teacher's and classmates' help.'

- I asked colleagues to comment on my lessons. Moira Laidlaw and Li Peidong, a senior teacher, offered positive feedback.

What have I learned from doing my research?

I have learned many things, including the following:

The relationship between students and teacher is important. Teaching for learning is about developing the right teaching methodologies as much as students' learning ability.

Action research involves self-reflection. It is not easy and takes commitment. You need to be imaginative and to care about everything you do. In the process of doing action research, I became more aware of my teaching because I paid attention to the educational purposes of each aspect.

I learned that just as life is worth living, action research is worth doing. When I tried new ways, and kept on trying, my teaching became wiser, more systematic and more enjoyable. When I compare my role to the role of a dancer, I understand that previously I dominated the stage and expected my students to be my audience. Now I have become an organiser, a director who helps the 'audience' to be actors and actresses themselves. They do the work, and I have more time to reflect on and record what happens in class and make an instant evaluation of my teaching. Though I now do less speaking in class, I spend more time preparing, and I ask myself questions such as, 'What do I want my students to learn? Which way would be better for them to learn? How can I help them to learn?'

Interestingly, out of this research a new problem has arisen. Students who were more proficient in English seem less motivated than before. I am wondering whether it is because of the attention I have paid to the lower-achieving students. So my next research question will be about developing differentiated teaching methodologies that enable all to learn according to their individual learning strengths.

CASE STORY 2: HOW CAN I HELP TWO STUDENTS IMPROVE THEIR CONFIDENCE IN LEARNING ENGLISH?

Gong Lixia

I am a teacher of English in the foreign language department at Guyuan Teachers' College. My research question is, 'How can I help two students improve their confidence in learning English?' In this report I outline my research, with special emphasis on the strategies I developed to help two of the lowest-achieving students to improve their confidence in my class. My research shows that these students have become more confident than before, and I produce evidence to support this claim.

My context

I have been a teacher of English for more than a year and a half in the foreign languages department of Guyuan Teachers' College. Even while still a college student, I had a vision of being a good English teacher and helping my students learn English well.

This was the first time I had taught a five-year English majors course. Most students in my class came from schools in rural areas, near the Guyuan municipality. For a range of reasons, they were not achieving well in English. Some could not even read a simple sentence correctly. Often they bowed their heads in my class. When I asked them why, they responded that their English was so poor that they were afraid to make eye contact. Two students, Zhou Peng and Gao Sheng, told me they were afraid I would ask them questions. I therefore decided that one of my most important actions would be to help the students improve their confidence, in order to make progress in English. I subsequently tried various strategies, and some students began to make progress. But Zhou Peng, Gao Sheng and several other boys remained the same, and I was at a loss how to help them.

By this time, some of my colleagues were undertaking their action enquiries into helping their students to learn English, supported by Moira Laidlaw. These colleagues advised me to begin my own action research and help myself to find my own answers. I followed their advice. Moira helped me to develop an action plan and work to it.

Here is how I put my plan into action.

What was my concern?

I needed to help Zhou Peng and Gao Sheng to develop their confidence. My research question became, 'How can I help two students improve their confidence in learning English?'

Why was I concerned?

Like many people, I believe that self-confidence is half way to success in language learning. Lack of confidence often leads to lack of motivation and interest, a situation that is contrary to the central idea in the New Curriculum, which emphasises active engagement through student-centred pedagogies.

How could I improve the situation?

I needed to find ways of helping my students to develop their confidence. I could best do this by appealing to the students' interests. Most students in my class are between 15 and 17 years old, and love being praised and encouraged. They also like competition. I therefore decided to do the following:

I chose Zhou Peng and Gao Sheng as key participants. Although their English is below standard, they are eager to learn.

I decided actively to encourage them. From their self-evaluation papers (handed in once a month) I had discovered that they were afraid of making mistakes, even though they knew many answers to my questions. The New Curriculum also advises teachers to encourage students to develop active language skills. I began to encourage them systematically. I said things such as, 'Believe in yourself, you can fly. Don't be shy, just have a try.' To my delight they began to put up their hands occasionally.

I began to praise them. When I was young, I liked being praised by my parents, grandparents, teachers and friends. I believe my young students are the same. Students will usually work harder when they are praised. So when the two boys got something right I would say, 'Good, very good, terrific, good idea, well done!' One day, Zhou Peng made the sentence, 'Can I talk with you?' I praised him, 'Good!' After a while, he put up his hand again and made another sentence, 'I can't speak English well.' 'Very good!' I praised him again. He sat down with a smile on his face.

I asked some more confident students to help the less able students. I met with the confident ones and reassured them that they would consolidate their own learning through helping others. They later began to help some students, including Gao Sheng and Zhou Peng.

I set up competitive games among my class. The New Curriculum requires teachers to design focused learning activities for maximum participation. Consequently, I often divide my students into eight groups for oral work. Reading practice is easy for excellent students, but difficult for less able ones. These games are organised according to rules that ensure that all students get an equal opportunity to participate and to succeed. Competition, however, is fierce. The winners are the group who achieve the most correct sentences in the shortest time. Both Zhou Peng and Gao Sheng tried hard for the honour of their group, and whenever their group won they were delighted, and celebrated by making faces at the other groups.

I initiated pair work, which is easier than group work. Each student helped the other in pronunciation and sentence construction.

I developed differentiated learning strategies, which is another requirement of the New Curriculum. I ensured that my questions were appropriate to individual students' levels of ability, so that they could succeed in their learning. Both students responded well to this strategy.

I decided to pay attention to the moral welfare of the two boys. I often talked with them individually after class. We talked about life and feelings, love and respect, their dreams and family situations. I encouraged them to overcome difficulties, understand others, respect others and also be self-respecting; and I mentioned how hard their families struggled to support their studies. My strategy seemed to work, because they tried all the harder.

How can I show that this situation has improved?

I have done so much, but how can I know whether I have really helped the two boys to improve their confidence?

Here are the standards I have devised to judge what I have done.

Do they participate in class actively?

Last semester, Zhou Peng and Gao Sheng were always silent. They never put up their hands to answer my questions. Gao Sheng always gazed at me as if at a loss. They now put up their hands at least twice in each class period. They discuss how to make sentences, and they correct other students' mistakes on the blackboard. They participate much more actively.

Do they finish their assignments independently?

Here, 'independently' means not copying from others. Last semester two of the boys' assignments were similar to those of several excellent students. I now devised strategies such as observing them closely to ensure that they were not copying. Sometimes I pretended to stand on the platform and read my book, but raised my head to observe Gao Sheng and Zhou Peng every now and then. They were either busy writing or discussing ideas with others, but neither of them was copying anyone else's work.

Do they enjoy their learning?

The two boys used to look very nervous in class. These days, the situation has completely changed. They lift their heads and sit upright with big smiles on their faces when they have learned something from others or followed what I've said. When they answer a question correctly, they sit down with a proud smile. They are very talkative when discussing ideas with others.

Do they engage in their own learning?

The two boys now ask me questions spontaneously about difficult words, phrases and sentences in the textbook. As noted, they have started to discuss questions with their partners, and do assignments by themselves. Zhou Peng has begun to take a dictionary with him and look up new words. This all suggests they have begun to learn actively. When I ask the class to write their answers on the blackboard, the two boys volunteer every time.

Do they accept responsibility for their own English learning?

I believe the two boys are more responsible for themselves now. When reading aloud, they correct any mistakes themselves. Their reading speed is quicker and they read more fluently. They love correcting others' mistakes too. Their handwriting has improved and they enjoy writing sentences and phrases. They never seem to lose heart.

Do my colleagues speak well of them?

Ma Hong is the oral English teacher of my class. She told me Zhou Peng and Gao Sheng have made great progress in oral English. Wang Ying, the phonetics teacher, told me the two boys have improved their pronunciation and intonation.

Has their confidence improved?

I surveyed my class to find out how they scored themselves in terms of confidence. From my findings it appears that the two boys have become more active, independent, engaged and responsible for themselves. My impressions are supported by my other colleagues' comments.

I believe I am justified in claiming that I have helped my two students to develop their confidence.

Who has helped me?

Moira Laidlaw, Ma Hong, Wang Ying and other colleagues have helped me. They visited my class and offered me inspirational advice. Students in my class have also provided rich information by monitoring the two boys' study. I helped myself too by writing my reflective journals and taking notes.

What have I learned from doing action research?

I have learned that doing action research takes patience, perseverance and confidence. It is creative and imaginative work, not an easy option, but a sensible way to go for any researcher. I am learning to be a better teacher.

While Zhou Peng and Gao Sheng seem to have developed confidence in English learning, they still make many mistakes in speaking and reading. For my next action reflection cycle I would like to research the question, 'How can I help the students improve their speaking and reading ability?'

CASE STORY 3: *IN LOCO PARENTIS*: SHOULD TEACHERS BE PARENTS TOO?

Lisa Percy

> Should I worry about what my pupils eat for lunch? What about the thin girl whose packed lunch I routinely find uneaten at the bottom of my waste bin? What about the boy I know spends his money on cigarettes? Or the girl who only ever eats chips and Mars Bars?

> Which of these cases are my concern and which are a matter for their parents? Increasingly, teachers are being asked to step into the parent role.
>
> (TES Friday March 21 2003: 25)

Teachers are often described as being *in loco parentis*. This translates as 'in place of the parent'. I am using this enquiry to investigate what this means to me as classroom teacher, tutor and Head of Year, the responsibilities it carries, and whether teachers should in fact take on the role of parent for any part of the school day. I am also curious about the views of students towards teachers taking some parental role in their education.

Central to this enquiry is my belief that the role of the tutor is vital to the development of students, both academically and socially. Also central is my belief that as Head of Year I have a responsibility to ensure that my team of tutors are using their undoubted emotional intelligence (Goleman 1995) to help all students in their, and ultimately my, care to achieve their full potential, in terms of both their exam results and their holistic growth as young people. These are my embodied values (Whitehead 2003), which I hope are evident in everything that I do. Through my enquiry I hope to clarify for myself how I live these values and contribute to the knowledge base of education by expressing, clarifying and communicating the value of *in loco parentis* as a living standard of educational judgement. Writing about my enquiry therefore becomes the 'story that I live by' (Connelly and Clandinin 1999).

I am currently a Head of Year 8 (students aged 12–13) in a proudly comprehensive secondary school where a large number of the students do not have a traditional parenting experience. Within my own year group, seven out of 225 students live with adults other than their parents, and 32 out of 225 live with only one of their biological parents. This has an impact on tutors. They have to be more than the adult who marks the register and chases absences. They also have to provide emotional and social support (James 2002). I am certain that caring relationships are the grounds for quality learning. I am interested in exploring the level to which this emotional relationship can be likened to that between parent and child, and whether the quality of this relationship has an influence on the academic achievement of students. Our students are the adults of the future and if they have not been supported in their emotional development by their parents or their teachers they have little chance of passing on their emotional skills to their own children.

My own experience of parenthood is positive. I have a strong, loving relationship with my mother and father. This has, I am sure, influenced my decision to become a teacher and pastoral carer, to pass on more than subject knowledge, and be involved in the holistic education of students, contributing to their moral education and helping them to become responsible citizens by providing a happy and safe environment in which they can learn. Initially as a tutor and more recently as a Head of Year I have been able to make a greater contribution towards this aspect of education.

In a review conversation with the Head Teacher at the end of my first year of teaching I raised my concerns and was challenged by him to do something about them. I began my second year of teaching as the only Head of Year in the school, responsible for implementing changes that had already taken place in many schools some years previously.

Gradually, with a lot of enthusiastic encouragement, the role was changed and form teachers were encouraged to become tutors and to have a wider responsibility for the students in their care. This change was beneficial to both students and staff. Improved relationships encouraged greater success as students were valued as people. This academic success in turn improved relationships. A positive cycle of emotionally informed success had been established.

Further work then led to the introduction and development of a tutor-led personal education programme and also the recognition that, through their contact and relationships with students, teachers were passing on not only their subject knowledge but also their own values and emotions. Teachers were developing strategies to encourage students to find their own responses to real-life experiences and situations.

From my current position as Head of Year, I am therefore faced with questions relating to the role of the tutor, including:

- How do tutors influence students?
- How can I as a Head of Year influence tutors to influence students?
- How involved should I become as a tutor?
- What is the relationship between all of these roles and the teachers' responsibility to be *in loco parentis*?

My research process

This is my story of my tutorial relationship with student Sam. Sam was placed in care at the end of August 2002 and so returned to school in

September from a foster home. He has social, personal and learning difficulties (SPLD) and has required a lot of support since he joined school in September 2001, but until recently my relationship with him had been relatively distant. From September 2002, however, I adopted the role of one-to-one tutor. As the relationship developed, I realised I was becoming to an extent his 'parent'. He would check in with me each morning when I would see that he had what he needed for the day. I often provided basic necessities, including on occasion breakfast, as well as an emotional start. He would then call in several times a day for support of one kind or another. In addition, we would spend one or two hours a week talking about whatever Sam wanted, often his home/family situation. At school Sam was 'happy' – he told me this at most of our sessions. He said that this was because 'You look after me and smile at me'. I hadn't realised that something so simple could make such a difference. This 'happiness' appeared to be translating to a calmer approach towards school and a more positive level of achievement. It also coincided with a change in Sam's care arrangements, where he had been moved to a longer-term placement with a foster carer described to me by Sam's Social Worker as a 'mother figure'.

So does the way that teachers act as parents in supporting students, particularly those students described by Bennathan and Boxall (1988) as providing 'special challenges', influence their achievement?

I enquired further by interviewing a group of students, who had experienced a number of tutors, about their expectations of the role of the tutor. Their answers reflected that a tutor should:

- look after the group
- take the register
- lead Personal, Social and Health Education, and
- be a trusted friend.

When asked about the role of Head of Year, the answers suggested a main responsibility for 'looking after'. Their comments included:

'Keeps us in a safe environment and teaches us about life.'

'Checks how we are doing and is strict when she needs to be.'

The students felt that both their tutor and Head of Year had an influence on their school day, their school work and their attitude towards school.

I then interviewed a Year 12 (aged 16–17) class, in more depth, about what makes a good tutor. They identified the following characteristics:

'enthusiastic, confident, respectful, a sense of humour, friendly, a variety of teaching methods, flexible boundaries between fun and work and most importantly they have to like children.'

I was interested in the focus on relationships and the fact that subject knowledge was not even mentioned. The students agreed that this was not a priority. When there was a positive atmosphere within the classroom and a positive relationship between the student and teacher, the subject or topic that was being taught was irrelevant. The group felt that the relationship above all else had to be trusting. Like a parent, the tutor's main responsibility was to help with social issues and problems within school. While the role of a classroom teacher was to inspire and help with exam results, the role of a tutor was to act as a friend. Sometimes students felt that they would even discuss more sensitive and personal things with their tutor than they would with their parents.

As a result of this discussion I decided that I needed to investigate in more depth the differences between the relationships with teachers and with tutors. I decided that a one-to-one conversation with a student would provide a different perspective and wondered whether the opinions and views expressed by the group of Year 12 students was representative of those held by all students. I interviewed one of my Year 10 (aged 15) students, John.

John felt that the relationship between tutor and student was closer than between teacher and student because of the amount of quality time spent together. This relationship had to be balanced and grounded in a set of negotiated rules that reflected humour and freedom together with a certain amount of control. According to John, 'To act as a parent in school. Keeping a close eye on us. Taking the time to understand us and talk to us about our problems.' He emphasised, however, that this role of tutor was carried out differently by different people, but each of the various styles of tutoring had positive influences on the students. This led me later to investigate various styles of parenting. You can read about these studies in my original extended essay (Percy 2003).

The role of the tutor therefore appears vital, because the way in which a student is tutored or parented whilst in school could have an influence on their levels of academic achievement. Considering this in relation to my own investigation, it is clear to me that students expect 'good' tutors to be the equivalent of 'good' authoritative parents. They should provide balanced levels of demand and response, high levels of support and the expectation of high levels of achievement and behaviour. It has also become clear to me that at times we tutors get this wrong and veer towards other parenting styles that have been demonstrated not to support students in achieving their best.

Conclusion

I am confident, from this enquiry, that the role of tutor remains vital in the holistic development of students. A parent of one of my students recently exclaimed that we probably knew her daughter better than she did. We saw more of the student than her parents did and probably had more conversations with her in the course of a day than her parents did in a week. Teachers have a responsibility to their students to act *in loco parentis* and reinforce the support that some receive at home. For those who don't receive any support, we go some way in providing what they need in order to achieve more than they ever thought possible.

CHAPTER 5

Evaluating your research: a case for teachers' self-evaluation

This chapter deals first with issues of evaluation and validity. It examines methodological aspects, such as setting criteria, selecting data, and generating evidence, and how these are supplemented by validation groups. It then goes on to consider issues of legitimacy, why teachers should conduct their own self-evaluations, and what might be the possible implications for their schools and beyond.

The chapter is in two parts:

1 Methodological aspects

2 Legitimating teachers' self-evaluations.

You have gathered your data and you are ready to generate evidence. You are also ready to show how and why your action research potentially has implications for others. How to do this?

1 METHODOLOGICAL ASPECTS

Evaluating your research is to do with establishing its validity, that is, the extent to which what you say is credible and trustworthy. It is about establishing the reasons why people should believe you. If you say that you think that the quality of children's learning experience has improved, how can you justify this claim? If you say that your learning has had a direct bearing on your practice, how can you show that link? How can you show that your claims are not a matter of opinion but are grounded in solid, authenticated evidence?

In traditional social science, there is often a demand for 'proof'. These days there is less emphasis on the idea of proof, even among the scientific community. It is now believed that the production of reasonably valid evidence is enough. It is impossible for you to produce concrete 'proof', and you should not even get into this language, but you do need to produce evidence. If you say your work is good, how do you justify this statement? If you are claiming quality professional practice, how do you demonstrate the validity of your position? How do you generate evidence?

Generating evidence involves three steps:

- Setting criteria
- Selecting data
- Generating evidence.

After taking these steps, you also need to think about establishing a validation group.

Criteria and standards of judgement

Evidence is found in data. Data and evidence are not the same thing. Data refers to all the information you have gathered about your actions, both your social actions in the world and also your mental actions in your learning. By the time you come to producing your report you will have amassed a good deal of data, and you now have to decide which pieces are directly relevant to what you are claiming to have achieved. Making choices about which data to use involves setting criteria.

We use the idea of criteria in all kinds of situations when we have to make a decision about the value or desirability of something. When shopping for a new coat, the criteria for whether you buy one coat rather than another will be something like the colour, fit and price. You will choose your coat depending on how well it meets your chosen criteria. You may well also make choices from a certain values perspective, that is, your standards. Some people are influenced by fashion and style, while others are influenced by cost. Our decisions are influenced by our standards, in this case, standards of style and fashion as well as financial standards.

The ideas of criteria and standards are key to generating evidence from the data. Which criteria will you use to help you decide which pieces of data to select as directly relating to your research issue and showing the issue in action? Which standards will you use to help you decide? Often the ideas of criteria and standards overlap, so don't worry too much about differentiating them. Just be sure you are confident about the idea of identifying criteria as a key component of your research methodology so that you can make professional judgements about your research. Here is an example.

A head teacher wants to test her understanding that the culture of her multi-ethnic school is non-racist. She can check her assumptions using quantitative measures. For example, she could check numerically whether all the ethnic groups are represented in, say, school council meetings or school plays. She could check how many parents representing different ethnic groups sit on the Board of Management. Quantitative issues of inclusion would be a core criterion. Inclusion is manifested in other ways, however, mainly through attitudes and discourses. How does she check whether attitudes throughout the school are inclusive? She could interview children from a range of ethnic groups and get their feedback. She could turn the whole project into a school project and include all members of staff, and invite them to interview children and get their feedback. This issue of course is highly complex, because it involves attitudes of teachers as well as children, and the degree to which people actually live their values or only talk about them. Values emerge as a guiding principle. The head teacher would need to make judgements about the extent and quality of ethnic inclusion not only in terms of quantity but also in terms of whether people really were living in the direction of their values or just paying lip service to them. In this case, the head teacher regards her inclusive values as her standards of judgement.

When you make a judgement about your research you also work in terms of how fully you are living in the direction of your values. If your research question is, 'How do I encourage children to learn?', your criteria will be to do with whether the children do in fact learn. If your question is, 'How do I help the children to improve the quality of their learning experience?', your criteria will be about whether the quality of their learning experience has improved.

Selecting data as evidence

The main way in which you can decide which data is relevant or not is to relate it to your research question. Asking the question, 'How do I encourage children to learn?', means that your criteria will be to do with whether children do in fact learn. Asking the question, 'How do I help the children to improve the quality of their learning experience?', means that you will search your data archive for all those pieces of data that show how you are addressing the question. Bear in mind that this data may challenge your beliefs about what you are doing and you may have to rethink things.

Perhaps, like many researchers, you gathered too much data at the start of your project. You may have been focusing on too many things, and may have gathered information about, say, children's playtime activities when you really wanted to focus on their learning activities in class. Selecting data means being disciplined about extracting only those key pieces that tell you something important in relation to your research question. Don't worry if you don't use all your data. The experience was not wasted, and the learning involved can be invaluable.

Generating evidence

Bearing your criteria in mind, you need to return to your data archive and find pieces of data that show the criteria in action. Perhaps students will say something like, 'This is great because I understand what I am doing now', or 'I went to the library because I wanted to find out more about this topic'. These statements would support your claim that you have encouraged learning. Perhaps they would also say things like, 'I really like coming to school now', or 'Can we continue talking about this in our next lesson?' These kinds of statement would support your claim that you have contributed to an improvement in the quality of their learning experience. You may also identify specific pieces of action on a videotape that show the criteria in action, or you may produce an analysis of classroom interactions that show all children contributing and demonstrating their capacity for enquiry learning.

These special pieces of data now become evidence. Their status as data changes to the status of evidence. The status changes, not the actual form of words.

Having selected your evidence, you now need to put it alongside your claims. If you say, 'I believe I have encouraged students' learning', you must place some evidence alongside the claim, perhaps in the form of students' words or a still picture from a video clip. You would place the video clip in your appendices or data archive. You can find examples of evidence that has been selected from data in the case studies in this book.

Validating claims to knowledge

A further step is needed to validate your claims to knowledge, in the establishment of a validation group. Although you have taken care to authenticate your data, and show the methodological rigour of your research by observing the tests of setting criteria and searching your data for instances of evidence, the claim still remains your claim and has not yet been subjected to public critique. This is an essential next step.

You need to convene a validation group. This is a group of peers, drawn from your professional circle, who will judge the quality of your evidence and assess whether or not your claims to knowledge are justified. A validation group usually comprises three to ten people, depending on the size of your project, and meets two or three times during the course of your research, initially to listen to or read your progress reports, and ultimately to provide feedback about its overall quality. While the main purpose of a validation group is to offer feedback about the validity of your research, the group also by implication lend legitimacy to it, that is, they show that they are taking it seriously, so it should be taken seriously by others and should be seen as holding significance for future practices and knowledge.

This issue of legitimacy is important because it has to do with power and politics, an area that involves you centrally as an action researcher.

2 LEGITIMATING TEACHERS' SELF-EVALUATIONS

The idea of legitimacy is different from the idea of validity, and is to do with who says a claim to knowledge is acceptable, and why they appear to be authorised to do so. It is often a case of who is in power. In 1600 Giordano Bruno was burned at the stake for claiming that the Earth travelled around the Sun. Although this claim was backed up with solid scientific evidence, it went against the teachings of the Church and so counted as heresy. The Church punished him for challenging official canons and discredited the legitimacy of his claims. It was a case of whose voice was more powerful rather than whose validity. The same kinds of situation are evident everywhere around the world today, when powerful groups relentlessly pursue their own interests, backed by immense resources of cash and technological achievement. Similar struggles for power are evident also in the world of ideas, nowhere more so than in educational action research, where the struggle for the legitimacy of practitioners' voices is a core issue.

In 1962 Raymond Callahan wrote his seminal *Education and the Cult of Efficiency*. He explained that, throughout the twentieth century, education had been greatly influenced by Frederick Taylor's theories of scientific management, which spoke of the need for efficiency in industry and business and later in schools. The mechanisms of scientific management were that people performed to a stopwatch, getting so many tasks achieved in so much time in the interests of greater productivity and more cash. Some implications were that educators were persuaded to focus on the operation of schools rather than the education of children, and teachers came to be seen as technicians whose actions were overseen by efficiency experts. This tradition continues today in Britain and elsewhere through initiatives such as performance management and new systems whereby teachers are paid by results (see Shuttleworth 2003 and Wragg *et al.* 2004). Underpinning this situation are issues to do with knowledge, especially issues of what counts as knowledge and who are seen as valid knowers (see Introduction). In the context of this present chapter, it becomes an issue of what counts as evidence, and who says.

The idea of evidence-based practice came to prominence in the medical profession, and was based on a scientific model (Thomas and Pring 2004). Outcomes were generally understood in terms of inputs, and evidence was based on statistical analysis. These ideas were taken up in education, and were welcomed by the existing dominant tradition that understood learning as the outcome of teaching, and that held that teaching itself could be understood and assessed through statistical analysis. The kind of evidence that counted in evidence-based practice was therefore accepted by the majority of the educational research community as statistical in nature.

Action research has seriously challenged this view. Action researchers believe that their practical knowledge is just as valuable for helping them make professional judgements as the conceptual knowledge of official researchers. The evidence they provide to support their claims to practical knowledge lies in the descriptions and explanations they offer in their accounts of practice. This evidence is authenticated by participants, and legitimated by validators, so their claims are demonstrated to have credibility. What is now needed is for the claims, and the evidence they contain, to be taken seriously by policy makers.

One of the key areas where these issues have come to the surface is in teachers' self-evaluation.

In previous times, evaluation tended to be carried out by an external agent such as an inspector. In many instances, such as Office for Standards in Education (Ofsted) inspections, this system remains in force. The inspector has a list of criteria by which to judge the degree to which teachers can demonstrate that they come up to standard. While this system is effective for those who do the inspection, it is not always valuable for schools (Slee and Weiner 1998). External inspection may identify issues from a technical perspective, but often entirely misses issues to do with context and emotions and, most importantly, with the values base of teaching and learning. Further, external evaluation may highlight such aspects from a diagnostic perspective and make recommendations about which aspects need improving, but it does not then feed back directly into practice. The supreme value of teachers' self-evaluation is that teachers themselves survey and critically engage with their own work, drawing on the insights of their peers and students, deciding for themselves which aspects they need to improve, and taking action on the basis of their own professional judgements.

The value of this approach is considerable, from a variety of perspectives:

- Teachers are in control of their own work. They decide on which aspects need to be addressed, on the basis of whether or not they are living out their values in their practice.

- Discussions about making judgements in the light of colleagues' critical feedback sets a tone of professional dialogue. Isolationist attitudes are broken down, and critical debate is encouraged.

- These kinds of sensitive but critical discourses inform the culture of the school. School comes to be seen as a setting for collegial discourse conducted by independently minded professionals. These discourses can inform the entire character of the school, reflecting in attitudes towards children and parents.

- The values base of education is prioritised. While attention is paid to the techniques of pedagogy, pedagogy itself is seen as a form of praxis.

- The individual self evaluations of teachers can lead to inclusive forms of whole-school evaluation (see Chapter 6).

These issues are generally agreed by the teaching profession as central to ensuring provision of an excellent education for children. They are not so regarded by those who are still persuaded by the ideas of scientific management and who are prepared to sacrifice educational goals in the interests of profit. This is one of the reasons why teachers need to become political, to regard themselves as intellectual and social activists (Sachs 2002), and to be prepared to stand up for their own knowledge. They need to find ways of letting their voices be heard, on behalf of themselves and also on behalf of those who are not able to speak for themselves.

SUMMARY

This chapter has addressed issues about how to establish the validity of claims to knowledge. The steps involved include setting criteria, searching the data for instances that show that the research question is being addressed, and presenting those pieces of data as evidence. It also involves developing validation processes, such as the establishment of validation groups, to show that the claim to knowledge is scrutinised carefully and tested against stringent critique. These processes are to do with demonstrating the validity, or trustworthiness, of the claim. Demonstrating the validity of a claim is different from having the claim accepted in the wider public eye, however, because acceptance involves power and politics. Some dominant groups may reject the validated claim for their own reasons. To establish legitimacy means that teachers have to find strategies to encourage people to take their work seriously. This involves both building up the evidence base of teachers' research, and also becoming political and developing clear communication strategies. These issues are dealt with in the following chapters.

> **CHAPTER 6**

Letting your voice be heard: a case for whole-school evaluation

This chapter is in two sections:

1 Making your work public

2 Whole-school evaluation for whole-school development.

The first section deals with methodological issues and explains how your work can contribute to a public knowledge base. The second deals with how whole-school evaluation works and the potential benefits for whole-school development and new discourses about education.

Now you need to make your research story available to others, on a small or large scale. Going public can range from telling other colleagues what you have done to writing a book. It is also essential to whole-school evaluation. If schools are seen as providing front-line services for children (Penny 2004), how do they show that this position is justified? League tables that appear as lists of figures, out of context and with little acknowledgement of the values base of education, do not say much about the school or the significance of the work. How do you communicate the ethos of the school in a way that does justice to its teaching and learning?

1 MAKING YOUR WORK PUBLIC

Having completed your data gathering and validated your evidence, you now need to let others know what you have done by producing a report. You can do this in different ways, using different forms of representation, which you can also mix and match.

Accounting for your work

Your report shows how you are accounting for yourself and your learning. You are making your account available to a wider public to test your claim to improved practice, and so that others can learn from you if they wish.

You need to be clear which audience you are writing for, and decide what your report will say (its content), and what it will look like (its form).

Content of your report: what will your report say?

Your report needs to have at least the following contents:

- *Descriptions*   narratives of what you have done, in relation to practice and learning.
- *Explanations*   why you did it and what you hoped to achieve.
- *Possible significance*   how your research can influence the education of others in your workplace and also at the level of policy.
- *Implications*   how your research can contribute to new forms of practice and theory.

Form of your report: what will your report look like?

Most reports are written. You can stick with writing, or use a dynamic form, or mix the forms.

Here are some guidelines. These have been found useful by teacher-researchers as they produce their first report. The researchers have explicitly structured their accounts using the guidelines. As their enquiries continue, and they gain more confidence, their narratives take on a life of their own, while still incorporating the guidelines. You can see this from the case stories in this book, and also from our websites, especially other accounts on http://www.bath.ac.uk/~adsajw/mastermod.shtml Have a look at the story of Siobhán Ní Mhurchú (2002) in McNiff and Whitehead (2002) (see also Ní Mhurchú 2000).

For a written report, organise your ideas so that people can see what you are saying immediately. Tell your story in relation to the questions you originally asked, writing in the past tense from your standpoint of reflecting on the research in the present.

- What was my concern?
- Why was I concerned?
- What kind of evidence did I produce to show why I was concerned?
- What did I think I could do about it?
- What did I do about it?
- What kind of evidence did I produce to show the situation as it unfolded?

- How do I show that any conclusions I am reporting here are reasonably fair and accurate?
- How have I modified my practice in light of my evaluation?
- What is the potential significance of my work?

You can use these questions as section headings in your report, if you wish. Go back to Chapter 3 for ideas about what would go under the section headings.

You can also organise your report using the following section headings:

Introduction

Introduce yourself. Say what the research was about, what your research question was, and what you have achieved (your claim to knowledge). Give a brief overview of the chapters or sections of the report.

Background to the research

Say why you wanted to do the research, in terms of realising your educational values, such as justice, freedom and creativity.

Contexts of the research

Explain the contexts of the research: your personal/professional situation, any relevant policy or theoretical contexts, or any other special issues that had a bearing.

Methodology and research design

Set out your research design (plan) in terms of timescale and other people involved. Say why you chose action research. Show that you were aware of ethical considerations.

Data gathering and interpretation

Say how you gathered data systematically and over time. Explain how you generated evidence from the data, and how you used it.

Potential significance of the research

Explain what potential contribution you are making to new practices and new thinking (theory). Say why your research is important.

Implications of the research

Say what you will do now in light of your evaluation and provisional findings. Say what other people also may learn, and the possible implications for them.

For further information and expanded versions of these frameworks, please see McNiff *et al.* (2005); see also the validated dissertations on www.actionresearch.net and www.jeanmcniff.com

It is up to you how you organise your report, within a context of who you are writing for, anticipated length of the report and, to a certain extent, other people's expectations. The first framework above lends itself to informal workplace reports, while the second may be more appropriate for formal reports submitted for accreditation.

You can produce your report in a dynamic form, also using multimedia technology. For example, video clips can be used as evidence to support your claims, which can show interactions more powerfully than the written word (see, for example, Farren 2004; Naidoo 2004a, b).

Contributing to the knowledge base

A knowledge base (what is known and how it has come to be known) is contained in published verbal, written and multimedia texts. The teaching profession needs a strong knowledge base so that all teachers can learn with and from one another. Teachers' stories can be shared easily using websites and internet communication.

Local knowledge bases can also contribute to the wider cumulative knowledge base. This is especially significant because:

- they present new models of practice that others can adapt or adopt for themselves
- they potentially influence policy
- they influence new understandings around educational and professional knowledge.

They present new models of practice that others can adapt or adopt for themselves

Case studies show how new practices can be developed. For example, evaluation used to be seen, and is still seen in some quarters, as inspection. New cases of self-evaluation show how teachers, individually and collectively, examined their work and took steps to improve it. Some examples follow, which are taken from higher-degree studies. We said in the Introduction that teachers can turn their classroom research into Master's and PhD degrees. Here is the evidence.

EXAMPLE 1

The earliest example is from a group of teachers who worked with Jack over two years (1974–6) to help their 11–14-year-old-students to improve their learning in mixed ability groups in science. This group developed a process of self- and democratic evaluation (MacDonald 1976) as they explored their questions with their pupils, 'How do I help you to improve your learning?' The report (Whitehead 1976) shows how they engaged in systematic action–reflection cycles, using video to explore differences between their intentions and the realities of classroom practice. It explains how their enquiries moved on as they responded to their experience of themselves as living contradictions in holding together the values that constituted their identity and the experience of seeing how these values were sometimes denied in practice.

EXAMPLE 2

The second example is an original study by John Loftus, a primary head teacher, striving to maintain his integrity in the light of incessantly changing education reforms.

John's account is based on a five-year research study (Loftus 1999), in which he enquired into his practice as a head teacher in the marketing of a newly formed primary school by asking, 'How can I improve my own leadership and management?' The study engages with Local Management of Schools (LMS) formula funding, open enrolment, opting out, standardised assessment tests (SATs), league tables and Office for Standards in Education (Ofsted) inspections. It describes how schools had been forced into competition with each other and consequently had to market themselves. He describes how he worked within these reforms, using them to provide enhanced learning opportunities for the students in the school. The research required long-term observation and reflection, and also extensive literature reviews of marketing strategies (both industrial and educational) and primary headship. John explains how he explored his educational values within the context of external pressure to initiate the process of marketing the school.

EXAMPLE 3

The third example is Tim Heath's account of his enquiry as a head teacher, which asks, 'How can I conduct worthwhile research into effective homework in my primary school?' (Heath 2004).

Tim explains how he discovered useful lessons from the natural sciences in declaring himself a reluctant convert to the methodology of practitioner action research. He describes the application of a practitioner action research methodology to his inquiry into effective homework and says:

'My account may be of interest to others undertaking school-based inquiries, particularly those for whom the action research approach is unfamiliar. It may also be of interest to established action researchers as a reminder of how very unfamiliar their methods can appear to prospective researchers.'

Examples also show self-evaluation processes by higher education practitioners working collaboratively with schools-based practitioners. For example, Joan Whitehead and Bernie Fitzgerald from the University of the West of England worked with Brislington School within the context of a four-year Training School partnership (Joan Whitehead and Bernie Fitzgerald 2004a, b). They explain how they moved from a traditional hierarchical approach, in which they 'passed on' the knowledge to teachers, to a collaborative approach where they saw themselves as learners who were in equal partnership with teachers who also regarded themselves as learners, and how this approach became the ethic between schools-based mentors and student teachers.

> Not only was the relationship between mentors and trainees different but so too was the relationship between university staff and school-based mentors, as we found new ways of working and developed new dimensions to our understanding and practice of partnership ... We confronted the hierarchy which had previously existed between ourselves and our school-based partners and between mentors as experts and their trainees.
>
> (Joan Whitehead and Bernie Fitzgerald 2004a: 5)

Other valuable accounts are by Pip Bruce Ferguson (1999) and Patricia Mannix McNamara (2004).

These kinds of initiative show colleagues coming together, discussing and critiquing their individual and collective work, making suggestions for improvement, and supporting one another. They show how critical engagement with new ideas can itself become the product; how committed staff engagement can lead to new organisational learning, which can feed back into new practices; and how the whole culture of the school can change away from inspection and towards cultures of engaged professional development.

They potentially influence policy

There is a new openness in policy-making circles towards teacher research, and considerable sums of money have been dedicated through initiatives such as the Best Practice Research Scholarships, on the understanding that teachers will produce results in relation to new learning. Here are some examples of how they do that.

EXAMPLE 1

Karen Collins undertook her educational enquiry, 'How can I effectively manage students' learning to take account of self-assessment within Modern Foreign Languages?', while teaching at Westwood St Thomas School in Salisbury, Wiltshire. Her account (Collins 2003) shows her responsiveness to her students' evaluations of her classroom practice in relation to students' awareness of their own progress. One of the strengths of Karen's account is how she focuses on the capacities of students within Modern Foreign Languages teaching to self-evaluate their own work, in ways that show their comprehension of the process and its outcomes. Another strength is Karen's responsiveness to the perceptions of her colleagues, to evaluations within the school's Ofsted report, to the school's improvement plan and to an internally conducted Faculty review.

EXAMPLE 2

Simon Riding's enquiry on 'Living myself through others. How can I account for my claims and understanding of a teacher-research group at Westwood St Thomas School?' (Riding 2003) explores the influence of an in-house teacher-research group at Westwood St Thomas School in Salisbury. In this account of his own learning, Simon considers the educational benefits of the existence of such a group for a school. He analyses his own work with the members of the group and explores the educational value of 'living through others'. He accounts for his professional growth as he matures through his dialogical relationships with other teacher-researchers. He also provides a brief account of how this group has developed and moved forward over the three years of its existence.

These examples show how teachers have come to understand their work as contributing to practice and theory. The need for this dual focus is high-lighted by John Furlong, currently President of the British Educational Research Association (BERA). He speaks of the benefits of collaborative working: 'By working collaboratively with teachers in their own and other schools and with those in higher education, and by deploying research skills themselves, teachers [are] able to use research-based knowledge in the development of their own practice' (Furlong 2004: 355). However, he urges teachers to regard their work as research, and to aim for high-quality research reports that will stand as the kind of evidence needed to persuade policy makers to take practitioner research seriously. This theme is also repeated by the new BERA Special Interest Practitioner Research Group, which aims to promote and disseminate practitioner research studies and bring together those who are interested in developing the field – see http://www.bera.ac.uk/sigs/sigdetails

They influence new understandings about educational and professional knowledge

Through the development of their knowledge base, practitioners can influence what counts as theory, and who should be seen as a theorist. Knowledge is not only about facts and figures, but is also embodied. When a teacher reaches a point with multiple options for the next action, which option does the teacher choose, and why? Decisions about how to act are not random, but draw on a teacher's vast range of experiential knowledge. Educational theory needs to be seen not only to be in scholarly books (for example, Peters 1973; Hirst 1983), but also to be embodied in the stories of teachers on the job. By producing their own living educational theories (Whitehead 1989), teachers are reconceptualising theory and showing its practical implications for the future.

Here are three examples, taken from PhD studies. When they undertook their studies, Kevin Eames was a classroom teacher, Ben Cunningham a teacher-educator, and Jackie Delong an educational administrator. Jackie's work is especially significant in showing the benefits for organisational development when an administrator also commits to studying her practice.

EXAMPLE 1

Kevin Eames asks:

How do I, as a teacher and educational action-researcher, describe and explain the nature of my professional knowledge?

The abstract to his PhD thesis says:

This thesis is an attempt to make an original contribution to educational knowledge through a study of my own professional and educational development in action research enquiries of the kind, 'How do I improve what I am doing?' The study includes analyses of my educative relationships in a classroom, educative conversations and correspondences with other teachers and academics. It also integrates the ideas of others from the wider field of knowledge and from dialectical communities of professional educators based at Bath University, Wootton Bassett School and elsewhere. The analyses I make of the resulting challenges to my thinking and practice show how educators in schools can work together, embodying a form of professional knowledge which draws on Thomism and other manifestations of dialectical rationality.

(Eames 1995)

EXAMPLE 2

Ben Cunningham asks:

How do I come to know my spirituality, as I create my own living educational theory?

The abstract to his PhD thesis says:

My thesis is a narrative which offers the following distinct and original contributions to educational knowledge, as I show originality of mind and critical judgment in connecting the personal with the professional in my explanations of my educative relationships with others.

I show how my living engagement with my God is enabling me to author my life and is part of the interweaving of my values in my educative relationships with others.

I show the meaning of my values as I explain my educative relationships in terms of how I dialectically engage the intrapersonal with the interpersonal.

I show how a dialectic of both care and challenge that is sensitive to difference is enabling me to create my own living educational theory which is a form of improvisatory self-realisation.

I show how my leadership comes into being in my words and actions as I exercise my ethic of responsibility towards others.

(Cunningham 1999)

EXAMPLE 3

Jackie Delong asks:

How can I improve my practice as a superintendent of schools and create my own living educational theory?

The abstract to her PhD thesis says:

One of the basic tenets of my philosophy is that the development of a culture for improving learning rests upon supporting the knowledge-creating capacity in each individual in the system. Thus, I start with my own. This thesis sets out a claim to know my own learning in my educational inquiry, 'How can I improve my practice as a superintendent of schools?'

Out of this philosophy emerges my belief that the professional development of each teacher rests in their own knowledge-creating capacities as they examine their own practice in helping their students to improve their learning. In creating my own educational theory and supporting teachers in creating theirs, we engage with and use insights from the theories of others in the process of improving student learning.

(Delong 2002)

The idea of practice as a form of theory, and the need for teachers to frame their practice as theory, is growing in strength. You can contribute by speaking about practice as theory as part of normal conversations, and encouraging others to do so too. Your conversations would promote new discourses at wider levels that policy makers could not fail to hear.

2 WHOLE-SCHOOL EVALUATION FOR WHOLE-SCHOOL DEVELOPMENT

When these ideas inform whole-school evaluation, schools can transform themselves into centres of educational excellence, where education is taken as a process of growth for all participants. Teachers come to be seen as critically engaged scholars whose theories of education contribute to new practices.

Getting to where this is regarded as the norm takes hard work and strategic action. Schools cannot expect the public simply to accept their word about the quality of their work without evidence. This evidence is in the real lives of teachers and students, and in the school's knowledge base in all its oral, written and visual documents as found, say, on the school's website. A school's knowledge base is its living articulation of its mission statement. While a mission statement of a school's educational intent remains on a wall, the knowledge base communicates the school's intent and its practical realisation.

Educating the public mind

Schools have a further task beyond their walls, which is to contribute to the education of the public sphere by helping people to become critical and think for themselves.

Given the culture we live in, and the power of the media, people sometimes assume that what they read and hear is automatically true, not seeing that messages tend to emphasise one thing rather than another. The success of schools is currently communicated mainly in relation to technical achievement using, say, league tables, which present information about a limited section of a school's life but which do not always show the reality of educational practices. This is part of the wider technical model that also judges teachers in terms of technical competencies. Putting accounts of practice into the public domain, through websites for example, to show how teachers hold themselves accountable for their work as part of normal school practice offers a more realistic story. The best websites show what is being done, and also explain why it is being done and what is aimed for. Presenting living accounts of practice gives people more in-depth and discerning insights into the practices of schools, and shows how schools can hold themselves accountable as morally committed communities whose major concern is the well-being of all participants. These accounts can shift public perceptions about how the work of schools should be understood, which can influence wider attitudes and promote new discourses that will in turn influence policy and feed back into practice.

SUMMARY

This chapter has urged teachers to produce quality research accounts that show how they theorise and hold themselves accountable for their practice. It has offered advice on what reports should look like. These reports can contribute to the public knowledge base, and they have potential for setting new directions for the teaching profession and for schools-based practices that will encourage sustainable learning. By producing their individual and collective accounts of practice, teachers can set new standards for whole school evaluation and improvement.

The idea of developing practices and theories that can inform new directions for the teaching profession is developed further in the next chapter, which deals also with disseminating your work.

CHAPTER 7

Sharing and disseminating your work

This chapter is in two parts:

1 Communicating the significance of your work for new practices and new theory
2 Informing policy.

Now you can describe and explain how you have created new knowledge about specific subject matters, and you can also show the process of your own learning. Your improved professional learning is a major outcome of your enquiry. Other people can learn from you about how to learn for themselves, and in turn encourage others to do the same. Your account is also important because it will stand as a piece of quality theorising that policy makers may want to draw on. You now need to disseminate your work so that others will see its value and understand how they can incorporate your ideas into their own.

1 COMMUNICATING THE SIGNIFICANCE OF YOUR WORK FOR NEW PRACTICES AND NEW THEORY

You can communicate the significance of your work and its implications in a range of ways, including:

● People and networks
● Publishing and presenting
● Projects and initiatives.

People and networks

Aim to disseminate your work to as many people as possible by linking into networks, both face to face and electronically.

Face to face

The most obvious place to communicate your work and its significance is in school, where you can help colleagues to frame their work as research. Staff meetings become a setting for professional dialogue, where teachers consider how the school is achieving its educational mission. Staff come to see themselves as implementing their own policy, not other people's, and conversations about practice shift from 'getting the buggers to behave' (Cowley 2001) to finding ways of enabling staff and students to grow together.

It is now possible for individual schools to link into a range of networked learning communities. The National College of School Leadership (NCSL), for example, has developed networks that connect practitioners at local level, and then connect local networks at regional and national level. Teachers have opportunities to share their learning at all stages of their projects and to get critical feedback, and case study evidence is now available. The NCSL currently operates only in England; others should follow its lead. For further information, visit www.ncsl.org.uk/nlc

Here are some comments from teachers connected through networked learning communities such as the NCSL:

'As a teacher coming from a PGCE background, networked learning provides the opportunity to gain invaluable experience from others, so that you can enhance your own limited experience. It provides essential support in undertaking your own research, knowing that you are developing capacity in explaining the validity of your research. You are able to discuss issues of practical concern and this breaks down the isolation that so many teachers suffer from' (Helen Flatman, Year 3 teacher).

'Working collaboratively with other practitioners has given me the opportunity to share, develop and reflect on points of my own practice. Practitioners need a time to share experiences and to develop insights into what drives their work and how they can constantly improve it' (Nick Heard, Year 3 teacher).

Although it is probably easier to link into an existing structure, you can also develop your own independent network. This happens all the time, such as inter-school or cluster meetings. The topics for these meetings can be about specific subject matters or about process issues such as management or school structuring. Many Local Education Authorities and other advisory boards arrange for these meetings.

Electronic networks

You can develop your network using electronic media. It is possible to contact anyone anywhere in the world through email, and thousands of schools disseminate their work by developing their own website and then linking with others.

Publishing and presenting

'Publishing' means making your work available to a wider audience, usually as a research report. Your report can be informal, written for colleagues or friends, or it can be formal, written for printed publication. It can be either in paper copy or in electronic form. Decide which is your favoured option and develop it.

Some people enjoy writing and others do not. Whatever your situation, writing takes commitment and organisation. You need to factor writing into your schedule and stick with it.

Producing paper copy

Here are some of the most obvious things you need to bear in mind when writing your report.

Writing for a reader

Many authors write for themselves, rather than for their reader. They sometimes assume that their reader already knows their research, which is not necessarily the case. You need to explain everything for your reader, even if it means stating the obvious. Ask a friend to read your report before you disseminate it. They may ask you to fill in missing gaps or to clarify things.

Writing for an audience

Decide in advance who your audience is. Is the audience your colleagues, your Board of Governors, or an academic audience? Different audiences have their own language. If you want your work to be given a fair hearing, you must write in the language of your target audience. Learning to write in what is sometimes a new language takes time and practice but it is entirely achievable.

Be prepared to edit what you write

People sometimes think they are going to get a text right first time, which is seldom the case. Even the most experienced writers spend hours and hours editing a few pages. Aim to produce a first draft of your work, and then go back and edit with discipline (frequently). Delete any repetition. Delete words and phrases such as 'very', 'surely', 'obviously', 'of course'.

Check that what you have written makes sense. If it doesn't make sense to you, it won't make sense to anyone else. Editing takes real critical engagement with your own thinking and articulation, which is hard work but essential.

Learn the conventions

Learn the conventions of good writing and of scholarly presentations. Check your spelling and grammar. Look at how other reports are presented for your target readership and adopt the same tone and style. Learn the conventions of referencing and citations, which is essential if you are aiming to publish in journals. Sometimes journal editors reject manuscripts whose technical presentation is faulty.

Organise your material

Writing for a reader means organising your material so that your reader can find their way through easily. Write in paragraphs and sections. Use section headings and other kinds of signposting to help them navigate. It is your responsibility as a writer to help your reader, not their responsibility to work out what you are saying. If they have to struggle to understand your text, they will probably put it down.

Electronic copy

The same issues apply if you are presenting your work electronically, using multimedia technology. You are still producing a text. You still need to be disciplined about presenting for a reader or listener, using the language of your target audience, editing your presentation, learning the conventions of presentation, and organising your material.

Organising is also vital in multimedia presentations, where you are using rich visual stimuli along with a written or oral text. People can take in only a limited amount of information at any one time, so ensure that you are presenting them with only that information that you want them to attend to. Leave visual images up long enough for them to take it all in. If you present text on a screen, read the text to your audience. Messages need to be integrated and synthesised. Let them hear and see that you are committed to what you are communicating. Explain the significance of your images to your audience, and show how these images should be contextualised in the whole field. Give people the information you want them to have, and then help them to make it their own.

Projects and initiatives

Opportunities exist for school-based action research initiatives, on an individual and collective level. Personal initiatives can often have unexpected spin-offs. Here are some ideas about how you can develop your own initiative.

Individually

Anyone can enquire into their practice. You just decide to do something about an issue that won't go away. Your project can be formal or informal, for your own professional interest or for accreditation. Colleagues or the whole staff can act as critical friends and validation groups. Sometimes, however, professional contexts are not supportive, so teachers need to find other professional groups as allies.

Sometimes one person's action research leads to greater involvement by staff and other groupings. Some years ago Mary Roche, a primary teacher in Cork, began teaching philosophy to her four- and five-year-old children. She undertook her Master's studies to monitor her work (Roche 2000), and has now moved to PhD studies. Her children displayed such remarkable capacity for critical thinking that Mary's principal invited her to conduct in-house, in-service work for peers. Teaching critical thinking skills has become part of every teacher's repertoire. Mary now conducts professional development seminars and workshops at national level, and her ideas are listened to by higher education institutions in Ireland. Similarly, Caitríona McDonagh, a primary teacher in Dublin, began investigating some 20 years ago how she could support her so-called learning-disabled students. She spent time and energy developing new pedagogies that would enable her children to learn in their own ways, as well as resources that would be meaningful and relevant to them. She formalised her studies through her Master's (McDonagh 2000) and later Doctoral studies. Like Mary, Caitríona's work has become well known in Ireland, and she is involved in professional development work at regional and national level. Both Mary and Caitríona know the importance of going public, and they systematically disseminate their work (for example, McDonagh 2003, 2004; Roche 2003, 2004).

Collectively

One of the best examples of a collective study is by Moira Laidlaw, formerly a secondary teacher in the north of England and a part-time lecturer at the

University of Bath (see Moira's writings on http://www.bath.ac.uk/~edsajw/moira.shtml). Moira was brought to China as a voluntary services worker, to undertake professional development work in Ningxia Province, one of the poorest areas in China. This was part of the national effort to improve the quality of spoken English among teachers and also to support them in developing new person-centred pedagogies that would be appropriate for the New Curriculum (Voluntary Services Overseas 2003b) (see Moira's story on pages 120–123). Working with colleagues in your contexts, you also can produce your stories of collective practice to show how you improved the quality of learning for yourself and others.

2 DEVELOPING YOUR WORK IN ORDER TO INFLUENCE POLICY

We now want to return to the issue raised in the Introduction about why teachers should do action research and how their work can contribute to debates about policy. We link this to the point that policy makers tend to develop and implement policy according to their own politically-informed motives, and draw selectively on published research to back up their decisions, which means they mainly draw on abstract theory. Teachers' research is still not widely accepted as theory creation. Teachers are still seen as engaging in schools-based professional development, not in the production of theory for educational sustainability (see Furlong 2000, 2004).

So what does it take to turn your practice into a form of theorising? It takes mainly two things:

- Making clear the evidence base of your claim to knowledge
- Your sustained commitment to understanding practice as a systematic research programme.

Making clear the evidence base of your claim to knowledge

We have said throughout that doing your research lets you make a claim to knowledge, that is, to say that you know something that was not known before. This claim has to be supported by authenticated evidence, which you extract from your data and submit to public testing and critique. It is important to explain why the data you offer in support of your claim is evidence and not simply illustration.

Generating evidence involves articulating which criteria and standards are used to make judgements about the evidence. In action research, those criteria and standards of judgement are related to the values that inspired the research. For example, if your project is about how you can develop democratic ways of working, the values of social justice and democracy would inform the work and would act as your standards of judgement. Do the pieces of data you have selected show you acting in a just and democratic way? If they do, and your critical colleagues agree that they do, those pieces of data can stand as evidence. Sometimes, however, it is not so straightforward, because the evidence may actually show that you were mistaken in thinking that you were achieving your goals, so the agreement you were seeking may not be forthcoming and you have to think again.

Our values are aspects of how we perceive ourselves in relation to others (our ontological beliefs). Our values are embodied in who we are and what we do, and form the bedrock of self-study action research. Bullough and Pinnegar (2004) say: 'The consideration of ontology, of one's being in and toward the world, should be a central feature of any discussion of the value of self-study research' (p. 319).

Producing evidence means searching your data to find instances of you living in the direction of your values, and making clear the link between your values and your practices. This means articulating your embodied values, and showing how you live by them. You articulate and communicate the standards you use to judge what you know and how you have come to know.

Your sustained commitment to understanding practice as a systematic research programme

Getting to grips with these ideas can take time. Although the ideas are quite new in the literature (Jack began writing about them in the 1970s), the educational research community has taken them up readily. Also, case studies did not exist until recently to show how the ideas could be used and incorporated into accounts of practice. Case studies are now available, thanks to pioneers such as James Finnegan, Mary Hartog, Ram Punia and Joan Walton, extracts from whose PhD thesis abstracts appear below, so the path for future researchers should be a bit smoother.

Here are those extracts, which show how teachers use their values as the standards by which they make judgements about their research and practice.

James Finnegan (2000) asks, 'How can love enable justice to see rightly?' He writes:

> In creating my own educational theory, I demonstrate how I have become a more reflective educational action researcher in developing and defining an original set of standards of judgement for judging my action research and teaching practices. These include my methodological, educational, and social standards of judgement. In helping to facilitate an expression of student voices in my teaching, as I seek to improve their learning, I enable my sixth form students and myself to engage in more democratic actions and more egalitarian power relations in the classroom, primarily through the elicitation/creation, greater enactment, and evaluation of teaching/learning communicative activities. In this, 'How can I help you to improve your learning?' is a question worth asking my sixth form students.
>
> My work also shows that I have become a more reflective practitioner as I dialogue with the writings of other educators whilst seeking to relate my values concerning democratic action and social justice to my classroom teaching.

Mary Hartog (2004) writes:

> This thesis is a self-study of a tutor in higher education committed to practice improvement. It is presented as a study of a singularity and an example of first person education action research. It is epistemologically and methodologically distinct in that it is based on my values as an educator and ideas about what constitutes loving and life-affirming educational practices.

Ram Punia (2004) writes:

> This autobiographical self-study presents my living educational theory of lifelong learning as an international educator with spiritual values including belief in cosmic unity, continuous professional development for personal and social development of life in general. The landscape of knowledge includes India, UK, Singapore, Hong Kong, Fiji, Samoa and Mauritius in several roles including a lecturer, teacher trainer, change agent in curriculum, staff, school development, a training technologist in corporate learning and a student in the University of Bath.

Joan Walton (2004) writes:

> If I know that I reside in the imagination of a loving compassionate intelligence, who desires me to live my story out to the full, and will give me full reign to do so if I can handle it, then I can respond to that, with no fear of consequences. I need not fear being adversely judged or condemned for what I do. Given the knowledge I have developed during the course of this enquiry, there is one criterion that I can reliably use to guide me; and that is that, in everything I think and do, I do it in the consciousness that I am interconnected to everything that is.

Bear in mind that this business of demonstrating the validity and legitimacy of practitioners' accounts as a form of theory generation is itself subject to attack. Researchers working in established traditions sometimes try to undermine practitioner research. It is important to counter this tendency. One way is by developing creative compliance, a strategy outlined by Barry MacDonald (1987). Compliance in this case does not mean giving in. It means being pliable, recognising the direction and force of the prevailing wind, and bending to withstand and move with it while finding new ways to grow. Some researchers have found ways of complying creatively in order to live with a hostile situation and still manage to show how they are living in the direction of their values, even when these are at odds with the values of the institutions in which they work. For example, Geoff Suderman exercised creative compliance when his classroom-based research was blocked by a university's ethics committee, so he studied his own learning from the experience (Suderman-Gladwell 2001). Sometimes this is all a practitioner can do, in their local context, while still aiming to contribute to other people's learning by showing how they have determinedly continued to value their own learning.

SUMMARY

This chapter has set out the need to communicate the significance of your work by means of networking, publishing, and developing your own school-based networks. It is crucially important to explain to others the significance of your work if you wish it to be accepted in the public domain. Policy makers listen to research that is recognised by the peer community as quality theorising, so if you want to have a voice in policy debates, you have to ensure that your work is of the highest quality, and expend energy in making it public.

The next case story is by Moira Laidlaw, who works in China as a volunteer with Voluntary Services Overseas (VSO). It is an excellent example of how one person can influence policy and practice on a massive scale. Such transformation takes time, although in Moira's case it has happened in just three years, a phenomenal feat. In September 2004, Moira's work was officially recognised by the Chinese Government when she was granted the State Friendship Award. The full text of the Award follows her story. It just shows what can be done with determination and courage. Moira will tell you that she had no intention of going to China until just before the event. Hers was a calling in the most profound sense of the word. Having responded to her call, she has achieved much on behalf of the Chinese people through education. We, Jack and Jean, are proud to call her friend.

CASE STORY 4: HOW CAN I HELP TO PROMOTE SUSTAINABLE EDUCATIONAL DEVELOPMENT AT CHINA'S EXPERIMENTAL CENTRE FOR EDUCATIONAL ACTION RESEARCH IN FOREIGN LANGUAGES TEACHING?

Moira Laidlaw

I am an educational volunteer with Voluntary Services Overseas (VSO) on my third year of a five-year project in a teaching college in rural China. In December 2003 Tian Fengjun, the Dean of the Foreign Languages Department in the college, opened an Action Research Centre specifically to enhance teachers' professional development in the local area and beyond. My job is Advisor to the Centre and over the next two years I aim to promote sustainable development there, which is one of the key aims of VSO's involvement in Chinese education (see www.vso.org.uk for further details). By sustainable development I am referring to a quality of development which can largely nurture itself and needs less outside help in order to flourish in the future.

Guyuan is one of the poorest cities in China (Voluntary Services Overseas 2003a) and suffers from its isolated location in the north west. China is about to implement its New Curriculum for the teaching of English, which requires teachers to develop their strategies from didactic to more student-centred methodologies (Voluntary Services Overseas 2003b). This is an enormous challenge to both teachers and students, who are used to being told what strategies to use, rather than developing their own. Over the last 15 years, the Beijing Government has invited educational charity workers into the country to help span the differences between Eastern and Western ways of doing things. The Centre aims to bridge some of the gaps between past traditions and current needs. It is the first of its kind in China so there are no precedents to guide us.

The department has about 40 members of staff, ranging in age from 23 to 50 years old. The majority are younger than 35. At present we have 29 undertaking their own self-chosen action enquiries and trying to improve practice in their classrooms. In addition, ten English teachers at a secondary school in the province are conducting their own action enquiries. Dean Tian Fengjun and I are currently editing a book of case studies entitled *Action Research and the New Curriculum in China*, which we hope to have published by an English language publisher in China (see www.actionresearch.net/moira.shtml for examples of case studies and earlier work in action research from the Centre).

One of my chief concerns as advisor to the Centre has been the promotion of sustainable development. As a volunteer and a foreigner, it seems crucial to me to embed deeper critical thinking skills and encourage intellectual challenges, especially to what I say and do, into the processes themselves, so that when I leave the research can develop in its own way. This has been partly successful (see website above for confirmation of this claim) and has been managed through the collaborative networks we have established both inside and outside the department. We have weekly meetings in two different groups during term time (the year is divided into two, rather than three, terms) and daily conversations about our research. We hold validation meetings for written reports to check whether what we are claiming is defensible or not, as well as helping the younger members build their professional abilities. We also have a system of classroom observations, in which the observer discusses the action enquiry with the teacher and then makes notes according to what the teacher needs to find out. These notes are subsequently kept centrally and are open to anyone in the department for information and ideas. We have also built a strong connection with Bath University's Action Research Group in England. Jean McNiff visited us for two weeks during the time of the opening of the Centre in December 2003 to help in the formation of the Centre. Jack Whitehead visited us in October 2004. Such visits lend a necessary outside influence, offer visibility for the Centre, and enable colleagues to exchange ideas internationally. It also takes the limelight off me.

Another key way in which I am promoting sustainability is to devolve power. As a foreign 'expert' I am expected to 'know the right answers'! Clearly this goes against the critical thinking skills required of action research processes (McNiff 1993). Therefore, in collaboration with Dean Tian, I have encouraged colleagues like Li Peidong and Zhao Xiaohong, both senior lecturers in the department, to shoulder some of the responsibilities of leadership. In addition I have encouraged younger colleagues like Ma Hong, whose account you can see in this volume, to take over the leadership of the less experienced researchers' group. So far they have discussed ideas, held meetings, borrowed books, and reviewed papers.

One of the most difficult aspects of promoting educational sustainability has been to negotiate with colleagues about the significance of practice preceding theory, and about their own ability to create living educational theories. In traditional research paradigms, theory comes first and this is what my colleagues expected me to give them at the beginning. I had to learn how to promote practice through rendering the groundwork safe, with ideas about action research, before expecting them to develop their own theories. We have so far enjoyed some success in publications. Significantly, Dean Tian has recently published an article in a national educational journal about our action research work (Tian 2003), which we feel will be helpful in promoting independence for the Centre in the future. It will help to promote our academic status and hopefully encourage others to come to the Centre for their own in-service needs.

In order to encourage sustainable educational development I have initiated what is now becoming a focal point of interest at the Centre. The case studies and reports, which have emerged from colleagues' research processes over the last two years, have revealed, we believe, the emergence of a new kind of action research. We are calling this new form 'action research with Chinese characteristics', and some of the case studies at www.actionresearch.net/moira.shtml already reveal some new ways of seeing research. We realise that action research has largely taken a Western research form, although it is beginning to achieve momentum in China with researchers like Professor Wang Qiang in Beijing and her recent book, *Action Research for English Teachers* (Wang 2002). However, it is our belief in the Centre that if we encourage something characteristically Chinese, then it is more likely to withstand my departure in 2006, as well as to grow in dimensions appropriate for the context.

Early indications suggest that our action research work is robust. However, over the next year I am hoping to work more closely with colleagues in communicating the significance of individuals and groups taking more responsibility for the promotion of values such as critical thinking, initiative and a clearer understanding of the processes of rigour in an action enquiry (see Winter 1989). Through discussions with others, I believe these aspects are still outstanding in terms of completing my facilitation of sustainable educational development in the Action Research Centre.

As our written work emerges we hope to publish in book and article form as well as on the internet. If any readers would like more information about what we are doing, please contact me at moiralaidlaw@hotmail.com

Here is the full text of the State Friendship Award to Moira, awarded by the Government of the People's Republic of China, October 2004

The State Administration of Foreign Experts Affairs, authorised by the State Council of the People's Republic of China, has established a state-level 'Friendship Award' to thank and commend the foreign experts for their contributions and dedication to the training of Chinese personnel as well as China's social development, and economic, scientific, technological, educational and cultural construction.

Since you came to China, you have achieved excellent success through your hard work and have won the appreciation and respect of your Chinese colleagues. What you have done has promoted co-operation and friendship between our two countries. With the recommendation of your host unit, the department, municipality and province concerned, the State Administration of Foreign Experts Affairs has decided to confer on you the 2004 State Friendship Award after the appraisal by the 'Friendship Award' Appraisal Committee. It is my great honour to inform you of this good news and I would like to express my warm congratulations and pay my high tribute to you.

Meanwhile, I would like to cordially invite you to Beijing to attend the award-giving ceremony. It has also been arranged for you to attend the State Banquet in celebration of the 55th anniversary of the People's Republic of China.

In conclusion, please allow me to give my sincere thanks to your family members, who have given you their support while you work in China.

I am looking forward to meeting you in Beijing.
Sincerely yours,

Wan Xueyuan,
General Director
The State Administration of Foreign Experts Affairs.

End word

Thank you for reading our book. We have enjoyed writing it, because we have been able to set out some important issues that have implications for us all. We have explained how practitioners can have a voice in policy debates, but that this privilege comes with a price, in terms of your own resources of time, energy and commitment. The more you present your ideas in a way that shows why they are important, the more attentively you will be listened to. This means producing research reports that can stand the test of rigorous critique. Although this sounds intimidating, it is well within your grasp. If this book has made sense to you, you will now have a clear understanding of what it takes to carry out an educational action research project and how to write it up. Granted it may take practice, but you will learn. Good teachers always were good learners.

We have great hope for the future. Our hope lies in each individual's capacity to exercise critical creativity in their own learning, and in their educative influence in the learning of others. The image of stars and evolving expanding spirals on the cover of our book aims to communicate our conviction that each person has the potential to influence what happens now and in the future in potentially unlimited ways and unlimited contexts.

We believe that everyone can do this. You can do it. You have the power and the potential to influence your own and others' learning. We also believe that this is a project that saves lives. Much scientific enquiry, such as the development of new medical treatments, saves lives in obvious ways. Enquiries into learning and the development of new ideas for improving social action and the education of social formations can be every bit as life-enhancing and, in some cases, life-saving as other forms. 'I saved a life today', says the doctor. Teachers can say this too.

Countless teachers, including those who have contributed to this book, show how they do this. Directly and indirectly, they save lives by enhancing the flow of life-affirming energy that carries hope for the future of humanity. You can learn from them, and do similar things in your own contexts. It is in your power, and it is up to you.

References

Apple, M. (1993) *Official Knowledge: Democratic Education in a Conservative Age*. New York: Routledge

Bennathan, M. and Boxall, M. (1988) *The Boxall Profile: handbook for teachers*. London: Inner London Education Authority

Bruce Ferguson, P. (1999) *Developing a research culture in a polytechnic: an action research case study*. PhD thesis, University of Waikato. Retrieved 26th November 2004 from http://www.twp.ac.nz/research

Bullough, R. and Pinnegar, S. (2004) 'Thinking about thinking about self-study: an analysis of eight chapters' in J. J. Loughran, M. L. Hamilton, V. K. LaBoskey and T. Russell (eds) *International Handbook of Self-Study of Teaching and Teacher-Education Practices*. Dordrecht: Kluwer Academic Publishers

Cahill, M. (2000) *How can I encourage pupils to participate in their own learning?* MA dissertation, Thurles, University of the West of England, Bristol. Retrieved 26th November 2004 from http://www.jeanmcniff.com/theses

Callahan, R. (1962) *Education and the Cult of Efficiency*. Chicago: University of Chicago Press

Cluskey, M. (1996) 'Feminist research and how it relates to my classroom experience', *Action Researcher* (6). Retrieved 26th November 2004 from http://jeanmcniff.com/stories

Cluskey, M. (1997) *How can I facilitate learning amongst my Leaving Certificate Applied students?* MEd dissertation, Dublin, University of the West of England, Bristol. Retrieved 26th November 2004 from http://www.jeanmcniff.com/theses

Collins, K. (2003) 'How can I effectively manage students' learning to take account of self-assessment within Modern Foreign Languages?' Educational Enquiry Module, University of Bath. Retrieved 26th November 2004 from http://www.actionrsearch.net/module/kcee3.pdf

Connelly, F. M. and Clandinin, D. J. (1999) *Shaping a Professional Identity: stories of educational practice*. London, Ontario: Althouse Press

Cowley, S. (2001) *Getting the Buggers to Behave*. London: Continuum

Cunningham, B. (1999) *How do I come to know my spirituality as I create my own living educational theory?* PhD thesis, University of Bath. Retrieved 26th November 2004 from http://www.actionresearch.net/ben.shtml

Dadds, M. and Hart, S. (2001) *Doing Practitioner Research Differently*. London: Routledge

Davenport, J. (2004) *Gender Awareness Action Research Project: an adult educational guidance counsellor's journey through gender awareness*. Draft report. Limerick: Mid Western Health Board

Delong, J. (2002) *How can I improve my practice as a superintendent of schools and create my own living educational theory?* PhD thesis, University of Bath. Retrieved 26th November 2004 from http://www.actionresearch.net/delong.shtml

Doherty, R. (2004) (in preparation) *Action Research Report*. Limerick: Mid Western Health Board

Eames, K. (1995) *How do I, as a teacher and educational action-researcher, describe and explain the nature of my professional knowledge?* PhD Thesis, University of Bath. Retrieved 26th November 2004 from http://www.actionresearch.net/kevin.shtml

Farren, M. (2004) *Developing my pedagogy of the unique as higher education educator: how can I co-create a curriculum in ICT in education with professional educators?* Draft PhD thesis, University of Bath. Retrieved 26th November 2004 from http://www.bath.ac.uk/~edsajw/arsup/mfabs.html

Finnegan, J. (2000) *How do I create my own educational theory in my educative relations as an action researcher and as a teacher?* PhD thesis, University of Bath. Retrieved 26th November 2004 from http://www.actionresearch.net/fin.shtml

Furlong, J. (2000) *Higher Education and the New Professionalism for Teachers: realising the Potential of Partnership*. London: CVCP/SCOP. Retrieved 26th November 2004 from http://www.edstud.ox.ac.uk/people/furlong.html

Furlong, J. (2004) 'BERA at 30. Have we come of age?', *British Educational Research Journal*, 30 (3): 343–58. Presidential address to the British Educational Research Association, 2003 Retrieved 26th November 2004 from http://www.bera.ac.uk/publications

Glenn, M. (2003) 'Multimedia, the celebration of creativity and multiple forms of learning.' A paper presented at the symposium 'Critical Debates in Action Research', University of Limerick, June, 2003. Retrieved 26th November 2004 from http://www.jeanmcniff.com/criticaldebates

Glenn, M. (2004) 'How am I enhancing inter-connections with ICT?' A paper presented at the British Educational Research Association symposium 'Have we created a new epistemology for the new scholarship of educational enquiry through practitioner research? Developing sustainable global educational networks of communication,' Manchester, September 2004. Retrieved 26th November 2004 from http://www.actionresearch.net/bera04/bera5.htm

Goleman (1995) *Emotional Intelligence*. New York: Bantam Books

Hartog, M. (2004) *A Self-Study of a Higher Education Tutor: how can I improve my practice?* PhD thesis, University of Bath. Retrieved 26th November 2004 from http://www.bath.ac.uk/~edsajw/hartog.shtml

Heath, T. (2004) 'How can I conduct a worthwhile enquiry into effective homework in my primary school?' Methods of Educational Enquiry Module, University of Bath. Retrieved 26th November 2004 from http://www.bath.ac.uk/~edsajw/module/thhome.htm

Hirst, P. H. (1983) *Educational Theory and its Foundation Disciplines*. London: Routledge & Kegan Paul

James, O. (2002) 'If only we graded mental well being', *Times Educational Supplement*, April 11th, p. 4

Laidlaw, M. (2004) 'How can I help to enable sustainable educational development in our Action Research Centre at Guyuan Teachers' College?' A paper from China's Experimental Centre for Educational Action Research at Guyuan Teachers' College (75600), Ningxia, PR of

China. Presented at a Monday Evening Educational Conversation on 12th July 2004 in the Department of Education, University of Bath. Retrieved 26th November 2004 from http://www.bath.ac.uk/~edsajw/moira/ml120704.htm

Loftus, J. (1999) *An action research enquiry into the marketing of an established first school in its transition to full primary status*. PhD thesis, Kingston University. Retrieved 26th November 2004 from http://www.bath.ac.uk/~edsajw/loftus.shtml

MacDonald, B. (1976) 'Evaluation and the Control of Education', in D. Tawney (ed.) *Curriculum Evaluation Today: Trends and Implications*. London: Macmillan

MacDonald, B. (1987) *The State of Education Today*. Record of the First CARE Conference. Norwich, University of East Anglia

Mannix McNamara, P. (2004) 'Developing caring pedagogical relationships with my Masters level students.' Working paper, University of Limerick, Limerick

McDonagh, C. (2000) *Towards a theory of professional teacher voice: how can I improve my teaching of pupils with specific learning difficulties in the area of language?* MA dissertation, Dublin, University of the West of England. Retrieved 26th November 2004 from http://www.jeanmcniff.com/theses

McDonagh, C. (2003) 'Presenting Voice in Research Practice.' A paper presented at the symposium 'Critical Debates in Action Research', University of Limerick, June. Retrieved 26th November 2004 from http://www.jeanmcniff.com/criticaldebates

McDonagh, C. (2004) 'Aware Teaching, Learning and Research.' A paper presented at the British Educational Research Association symposium 'Have we created a new epistemology for the new scholarship of educational enquiry through practitioner research? Developing sustainable global educational networks of communication', Manchester, September, 2004. Retrieved 26th November 2004 from http://www.bath.ac.uk/~edsajw/bera04/bera2.htm

McNamee, M. and Bridges, D. (2002) (eds) *The Ethics of Educational Research*. Oxford: Blackwell

McNiff, J. (1989) *An explanation for an individual's educational development through the dialectic of action research*. PhD thesis, University of Bath

McNiff, J. (1993) *Teaching as Learning: an action research approach*. London: Routledge

McNiff, J. with J. Whitehead (2002) *Action Research: principles and practice* (second edition). London: RoutledgeFalmer

McNiff, J. and Whitehead, J. (2005) *All you need to know about action research*. London: Sage

McNiff, J., Lomax, P. and Whitehead, J. (2003) *You and Your Action Research Project* (second edition). London: RoutledgeFalmer

Naidoo, M. (2004a) 'How can I use creative process to improve my practice as a facilitator of healthcare?' A paper presented at the British Educational Research Association symposium 'Have we created a new epistemology for the new scholarship of educational enquiry through practitioner research? Developing sustainable global educational networks of communication', Manchester, September 2004. Retrieved on 25th November 2004 from http://www.bath.ac.uk/~edsajw/bera04/bera4.htm

Naidoo, M. (2004b) *I am because we are: how can I improve my practice? The emergence of a living theory of responsive practice*. PhD thesis to be submitted January 2005, University of Bath. Retrieved 26th November 2004 from http://www.bath.ac.uk/~edsajw/arsup/mnabs0304.htm

Ní Mhurchú, S. (2002) 'How can I improve my practice as a teacher in the area of assessment through the use of portfolios?' in J. McNiff with J. Whitehead *Action Research: Principles and Practice* (second edition). London: RoutledgeFalmer

Nugent, M. (2000) *How can I raise the level of self-esteem of second year Junior Certificate School Programme students and create a better learning environment?* MEd dissertation, Dublin, University of the West of England, Bristol. Retrieved 26th November 2004 from http://www.jeanmcniff.com/theses

Parlett, M. and Hamilton, D. (eds) (1977) *Beyond the Numbers Game.* Basingstoke: Macmillan Education

Penny, R. (2004) 'Supporting Practitioners' Enquiries.' A paper presented at the Teacher Researcher Conference, St Mary's University College, Twickenham, September 2004

Percy, L. (2003) 'In Loco Parentis: should teachers be parents too?' Educational Enquiry Module, Master's Programme, University of Bath. Retrieved 26th November 2004 from http://www.bath.ac.uk/~edsajw/module/lpparentis.htm

Peters, R. S. (1973) *The Philosophy of Education.* Oxford: Oxford University Press

Potts, M. (2002) 'What methods of enquiry can I use to live out my democratic values more fully?' Educational Enquiry module, Master's Programme, University of Bath. Retrieved 26th November 2004 from http://www.actionresearch.net/module/mpmee.htm

Punia, R. (2004) *My CV is my curriculum: the making of an international educator with spiritual values.* Ed.D. thesis, University of Bath. Retrieved 26th November 2004 from http://www.bath.ac.uk/~edsajw/punia.shtml

Riding, S. (2003) *Living myself through others. How can I account for my claims and understanding of a teacher-research group at Westwood St Thomas School?* MA dissertation, University of Bath. Retrieved 26th November 2004 from http://www.actionresearch.net/module/srmadis.pdf

Robson, C. (2002) *Real World Research* (second edition). Oxford: Blackwell

Roche, M. (2000) *How can I improve my practice so as to help my pupils to philosophise?* MA dissertation, Cork, University of the West of England, Bristol. Retrieved 26th November 2004 from http://www.jeanmcniff.com/theses

Roche, M. (2003) 'Setting the "what if?" free: some theoretical perspectives on talking and thinking in an infant classroom' in N. Hayes and M. Kernan (eds) *Transformations: theory and practice in early education: Conference Proceedings of l'Organisation Mondiale pour l'Education Préscolaire*, University College Cork, April (in preparation)

Roche, M. (2004) Progress report for PhD studies. University of Limerick, Limerick

Sachs, J. (2002) *The Activist Teaching Profession.* Buckingham: Open University Press

Said, E. (1975) *Beginnings: Intention and Method.* London: Granta Books

Schön, D. (1995) 'Knowing-in-action: the new scholarship requires a new epistemology.' *Change*, November–December: 27–34.

Shulman, L. S. (2002) 'Forgive and Remember: The Challenges and Opportunities of Learning from Experience.' *Launching the Next Generation of New Teachers Symposium Proceedings.* New Teacher Centre at the University of California, Santa Cruz, January

Shuttleworth, D. (2003) *School Management in Transition.* London: RoutledgeFalmer

Slee, R. and Weiner, G. (1998) *School Effectiveness for Whom?* London: Falmer

Steinberg, S. and Kincheloe, J. (1998) *Students as researchers: creating classrooms that matter.* London: Falmer

Suderman-Gladwell, G. (2001) *The Ethics of Personal, Narrative, Subjective Research.* MA dissertation, Brock University, Ontario. Retrieved 26th November 2004 from http://www.bath.ac.uk/~edsajw/values/gsgma.PDF

Sullivan, B. (2003) 'Democratising practice as a means towards achieving social justice'. A paper presented at the symposium 'Critical Debates in Action Research', University of Limerick, June 2003

Sullivan, B. (2004) 'The transformative potential of an educational practitioner's engagement in emancipatory practices. A paper presented at the British Educational Research Association symposium 'Have we created a new epistemology for the new scholarship of educational enquiry through practitioner research? Developing sustainable global networks of communication, Manchester, September 2004. Retrieved 26th November 2004 from http://www.bath.ac.uk/~edsajw/bera04/bera2.htm

Thomas, G. and Pring, R. (2004) *Evidence-Based Practice in Education.* Maidenhead: Open University Press

Tian F. (2003) 'Educational Action Research and Creativity in Foreign Languages Teaching' in *Foreign Languages Teaching Journal,* Xi'an, November/December

Tian, F. and Laidlaw, M. (2004) *Action Research and the New Curriculum in China: case studies and reports in the teaching of English* (in preparation)

Voluntary Services Overseas (2003a) 'In country profile.' VSO, Beijing

Voluntary Services Overseas (2003b) 'What's new about the New Curriculum?' Newsletter, VSO, Beijing

Walton, J. (2004) *Developing a Science of Consciousness in the Service of Love, Peace and Wholeness.* Draft PhD thesis, to be submitted to the University of Bath

Wang, Q. (2002) *Action Research for English Teachers.* Beijing: Foreign Languages Press

Wenger, E. (1998) *Communities of Practice: learning, meaning, identity.* Cambridge: Cambridge University Press

Whitehead, Jack (1976) *Improving Learning for 11–14 Year Olds in Mixed Ability Science Groups.* Swindon: Wiltshire Curriculum Development Centre. Retrieved 26th November 2004 from http://www.actionresearch.net/writings/ilmagall.pdf

Whitehead, Jack (1989) 'Creating a living educational theory from questions of the kind, "How do I improve my practice?" ' *Cambridge Journal of Education* 19 (1): 137–53. Retrieved 26th November 2004 from http://www.bath.ac.uk/~edsajw/writings/livtheory.html

Whitehead, Jack (2000) 'How do I improve my practice? Creating and legitimating an epistemology of practice.' *Reflective Practice* 1 (1): 91–104

Whitehead, Jack (2003) 'Creating our living educational theories in teaching and learning to care: Using multi-media to communication the meanings and influence of our embodied educational values.' *Teaching Today for Tomorrow* 19: 17–20. Retrieved 26th November 2004 from http://www.70aks.org/ttt/ttt19.htm

Whitehead, Jack (2004a) 'What counts as evidence in the self-studies of teacher education practices?' in J. J. Loughran, M. L. Hamilton, V. K. LaBoskey and T. Russell (eds) *International Handbook of Self-Study of Teaching and Teacher Education Practices.* Dordrecht: Kluwer Academic Publishers

Whitehead, Jack (2004b) 'Action Research Expeditions: Do action researchers' expeditions carry hope for the future of humanity? How do we know? An enquiry into reconstructing educational theory and educating social formations.' Retrieved 26th November 2004 from http://www.arexpeditions.montana.edu/articleviewer.php?AID=80)

Whitehead, Joan (2003) 'The Future of Teaching and Teaching in the Future: a vision of the future of the profession of teaching: making the possible probable.' Keynote address to the

Standing Committee for the Education and Training of Teachers Annual Conference, Dunchurch, October 2003. Retrieved 26th November 2004 from http://www.bath.ac.uk/~edsajw/evol/joanw_files/joanw.htm

Whitehead, Joan and Fitzgerald, B. (2004a) 'Experiencing and evidencing learning: new ways of working with mentors and trainees in a Training School partnership,' A paper presented at the American Educational Research Association symposium 'The transformative potentials of individuals' collaborative self-studies for sustainable global educational networks of communication', San Diego, April 2004. Retrieved 26th November 2004 from http://www.bath.ac.uk/~edsajw/multimedia/jwbfaera04.htm

Whitehead, Joan and Fitzgerald, B. (2004b) 'New ways of working with mentors and trainees in a training school partnership as practitioner-researchers.' A paper presented at the British Educational Research Association symposium 'Have we created a new epistemology for the new scholarship of educational enquiry through practitioner research? Developing sustainable global networks of communication.' Manchester, September 2004. Retrieved 26th November 2004 from http://www.bath.ac.uk/~edsajw//bera04/bera3.htm

Winter, T. (1989) *Learning from Experience*. London: Falmer

Wragg, E., Haynes, G. S., Wragg, C. M. and Chamberlain, R. P. (2004) *Performance Pay for Teachers*. London: RoutledgeFalmer

Zeni, J. (2001) *Ethical Issues in Practitioner Research*. New York: Teachers College Press

Index